Bike Tours
In Southern Arizona

Bike Tours
In Southern Arizona

by Philip Varney
with Mort Solot

maps by James M. Davis
photographs by the Author

Breakaway Press
4764 E. 10th St.
Tucson, Arizona 85711

ISBN 0-9628461-0-4

Printed in the United States of America
by Post Litho Printing

for Ned Mackey

Other Books by Philip Varney:

ARIZONA'S BEST GHOST TOWNS, Northland Press, 1980
NEW MEXICO'S BEST GHOST TOWNS, New Mexico Press, 1987
SOUTHERN CALIFORNIA'S BEST GHOST TOWNS, Oklahoma Press, 1990

Acknowledgments

Many thanks to Ed Stiles, who wrote the original text of this book; to Mort Solot, my friend and riding guru; to cycling companions Howard Goldwyn, Tom Bartlett, Richard Corvo, George Jacoby, Mary Ann Mead, Russell Mead, Julie Melson, Trevor Street, Jack Levy, Ralph Phillips, Bob Swaim, Ted Gantt, Benn Isaacman, Ron Adler, Drew Palmer, Helen Rosen, Bill Drum, Darryl Day, and Janet Varney, who suggested new rides, helped fix flats, shared centuries, ferried sag wagons, and provided unlimited support; to Jim Fiegen of Victor Racing Bicycles, who built me a truly remarkable bike; to Alan Fischer, Norman Kibble, Matt Freeman, Phil Bryson and Tom Tease, who gave me technical advice and racing information; to Jim Carlson and Chuck Kohler, who taught me essential bicycle maintenance; to Chris Ziegler of the University of Arizona map room, who tirelessly helps me in all my books and articles; to Dale Mann, Dave McDonald, and Jim Madden, who provided word processing expertise; to Mike Davis, who drew another great set of maps; and, most of all, to friend and fellow cyclist Ned Mackey, who got me out of my chair and onto a bike and who served as unofficial editor of this book long before he knew it was dedicated to him.

Contents

Introduction

Why a new book? The volume in your hands is a complete rewrite of a 1980 version of the same title. Since that time, much has changed in Southern Arizona: roads have been paved, routes altered, and streets added. Thousands more people call themselves cyclists than in 1980, and the animal known as the Mountain Bike has entered our lives.

Despite all those changes, Ed Stiles and Mort Solot's original book remains an excellent place to start for a rewrite, so when Ed and Mort asked me to re-do the original, I simply tried to improve an already good product.

Why me? In 1980 Mort Solot was taking a class I taught at the University of Arizona called "Ghost Towns of the West." We were on a field trip to the Tombstone area, standing at Brunckow's Cabin. Would I mind, Mort asked, if he used portions of my Arizona ghost town book for a bicycling book he was working on. I was not a cyclist— hadn't ridden one for probably 25 years. I looked at the desolate place where we were standing and asked if he planned to send cyclists out into this country. When he said yes, I remember thinking that here was this pleasant, intelligent fellow who seemed so reliable and responsible, but now I knew he was clearly insane. Send cyclists out on the Charleston Road? Hah!

By 1981 Ed and Mort's book had become my bible. I was riding hundreds of miles per month and taking long, looping tours with the book in my jersey pocket. I have a particular fondness for that original volume and bet that many of you do, too. Mort and I have probably cycled 3,000 miles together, and we have ridden on every road in this book.

So what's new about this edition? This 1991 revision has over 50 road and mountain bike rides; the original had 18. The maps and text now give more specific mileage (because in 1980 nobody had a cyclocomputer) and also feature important elevations. The chapters in the revision radiate from Tucson, so the first chapter concerns the immediate Tucson area, and the sixth ventures to Willcox. The last two chapters contain suggestions for mountain

1

bike rides, trips I've been making since I bought my first mountain bike in 1982.

What's missing from the first book? This version does not give advice on repairs, clothing, or equipment and does not provide local crosstown routes in Tucson. The emphasis here is on touring, not commuting.

But what if I'm a cycling commuter? So am I. But you can get much more useful and complete information on commuting from two excellent and free sources: The Tucson Bicycling Map, available from most bike stores or by calling 628-5313; and the University of Arizona Campus Bicycle Guide, available at many spots on campus or by calling 621-8751 or 621-1800. Since commuting information will change more often than touring data will, their maps and brochures will be updated more frequently than this book and will, therefore, remain more current.

How about additional information? The principal sources for this book, in addition to thousands of miles of riding, include:

Bike Tours of Southern Arizona, by Ed Stiles and Mort Solot

Arizona's Names (X Marks the Place), by Byrd Howell Granger

Historical Atlas of Arizona, by Henry P. Walker and Don Bufkin

Arizona's Best Ghost Towns, by Philip Varney

The last is presently out of print but readily available in libraries and occasionally in used book stores. You have my permission to photocopy anything in that book that would be of help to you.

An important warning — This book gives honest information about each of the rides, especially when hazardous conditions could exist. But remember: This is a terrific sport, but it remains a potentially dangerous one. I can't name one cyclist who rides regularly who hasn't fallen at least once. Often the fall isn't even the rider's fault: I have ended up on the hood of a car that turned in front of me. So **please** wear a helmet, watch traffic at all times, check road conditions constantly, and expect the unexpected. And please do not attempt distances that are beyond your capabilities.

A final suggestion — Before you begin a ride, read the text for that ride in its entirety as it may have information that you'll need to know before you go (e.g., on one ride, it's important to have a lock; another suggests carrying binoculars).

But most of all, I wish you thousands of miles of great cycling.

—P.V.

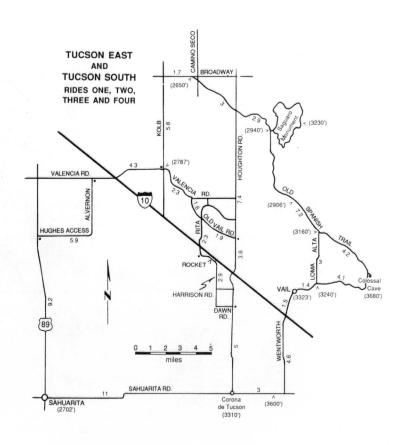

**TUCSON EAST
AND
TUCSON SOUTH**

RIDES ONE, TWO,
THREE AND FOUR

CAMINO SECO

BROADWAY
1.7
(2650')

3

2.9
(2940')

Saguaro
Monument
< (3230')

KOLB
5.8

(2787')
4.3

VALENCIA RD.

VALENCIA
2.3

RD.

OLD

SPANISH

(2906')

7.2

(3160') >

TRAIL
4.2

10

HOUGHTON RD.

7.4

ALVERNON

HUGHES ACCESS
5.9

RITA
2.3

OLD VAIL RD.
1.9

1.9

3.8

ALTA
LOMA

3

4.1

Colossal
Cave
(3680')

ROCKET

2.9

VAIL
1.5

1.4
^
(3323')

^
(3240')

HARRISON RD.

DAWN
RD.

N

89
9.2

0   1   2   3   4   5
miles

5

WENTWORTH
4.6

SAHUARITA RD.
11

SAHUARITA
(2702')

Corona
de Tucson
(3310')

3

^
(3600')

CHAPTER ONE
Day Trips from Tucson

The Tucson cyclist is fortunate indeed: he or she has countless excellent rides emanating in all directions from the city. Many routes are on low-traffic rural roads, some use major highways with good shoulders or bike lanes, but a few —alas— must proceed for at least part of the route along less desirable streets. Nevertheless, I consider Tucson's overall riding conditions to be better than many major western cities, where the rider is a stranger in a dangerous, strange land.

This chapter introduces you to thirteen rides, but one of the benefits of taking them is that they will open up countless variations for you. I try to take one new ride per week, even if it's just reversing directions or trying out a different side street. If you'll do the same, you'll come up with favorites in addition to the rides that follow.

Chapter One begins with the seminal bicycle ride of Tucson and radiates with the compass.

Tucson East

Ride One — Old Spanish Trail and Saguaro National Monument East (19 miles)

Without question Tucson's most popular ride, this is known simply as "The Monument Ride." It's also an excellent test for the novice rider who wants to know which rides to attempt in this book; when you can do this ride easily, you're ready for bigger challenges.

Old Spanish Trail — I like to avoid using the car to transport bikes wherever practical, so I ride from my house, in the Broadway-Swan area, out Broadway to Old Spanish Trail (4.8 miles). Many riders, however, park in the lots of a restaurant or a preschool just south of the intersection. The mileage given is for riders starting at this intersection (elev. 2650').

For the first three miles from Broadway, you have bike lanes on both sides of the road and a separate paved path that has become used increasingly by pedestrians. I recommend the road lane. The route is almost entirely uphill to the entrance to the monument; think about how enjoyable the return will be. At this writing, the bike lane ends at Houghton Road. The law says you can stay on Old Spanish Trail, but it has no shoulder at all, and many drivers resent your using the road when there is an alternate lane (the separate paved path that began at Broadway). I suggest you avoid the motorists' ire and join the pedestrians even if the law is on your side. But be careful and watch for dogs on long leashes, baby carriages, etc. You'll arrive at the entrance to the Monument (elev. 2940') at 5.9 miles from Broadway (or 10.7 miles from mid-town Tucson).

Saguaro National Monument (East) — Here is the best short-loop ride in Southern Arizona. This nine-mile stretch of desert beauty, in addition to the saguaro, contains hundreds of varieties of Sonoran flora as well as abundant wildlife. The bicycle approaches so quickly and slides by so silently that the rider can see many more animals than either a motorist or a hiker. In ten years of riding the Monument, I've seen deer, javelina, gila monsters, tarantulas, and even

On the back side of Saguaro National Monument East

rattlesnakes. But during tourist season you'll also encounter motorhomes and slow-moving, unpredictable drivers ("Stop, Harold! There's a cactus!"). My belief is that cars, runners, and other cyclists pose far more of a problem than wildlife. Ride the loop carefully.

The Monument staff has done a wonderful job of accommodating cyclists: you'll see a bike ramada on your left with bike racks, benches, and cold water. Since they've been so thoughtful, repay them by obeying a simple request: don't take your bike up to the restrooms at the main building.

The fee for entering the Monument loop is, at this writing, $1.00 for cyclists. Devotees buy the yearly pass for $10.00. Be sure to obey the two stop signs inside the park; cyclists have been cited and fined for ignoring them.

Riding the Loop — *Warning:* The first downhill on the loop can be just plain treacherous. A (helmetless) cyclist has died there. Please take heed of the caution signs and proceed slowly. After the first rollercoaster, the loop settles into a remarkably enjoyable jaunt—more downhill than up for the first 3 miles, then two stiff climbs at the halfway point (highest elev. 3230'), and then more rollercoaster riding. If you arrive early, you can beat the car traffic and feel as if you have the place all to yourself.

If you are new to cycling, don't feel embarrassed if you have to get off and catch your breath or even walk the bike uphill. When I first rode the loop in 1981, my cohort Mort Solot (a cyclist of many years before I started) chugged past as I was sucking wind (for the third time) on the big hill. As I am about twenty years Mort's junior, I was more than a little abashed. I vowed I would never again have to stop unless I wanted to enjoy the scenery.

When you come to your first stop sign, you can take a right and return to the entrance or take the road to your left for about .5 miles to the picnic area. This is a favorite breakfast location for scout troops on bike outings.

You'll have a second stop sign at the end of the loop. Turn left to leave the monument, or consider what I love to do on a gorgeous morning: turn right and take another loop.

Ride Two — The Colossal Cave Loop (38 miles)

Ride One is "The Monument" to Tucson cyclists; Ride Two is simply "The Cave," as in a typical opening of a conversation between two friends meeting at Broadway and Old Spanish Trail: "You doing the Monument?" "Yeah, and the Cave."

To ride the Colossal Cave Loop, first follow the directions of Ride One to Saguaro National Monument. Then either go in and ride the Loop or continue on Old Spanish Trail. The bike path ends at the Monument, but a shoulder continues to the Cave.

Rincon Valley — About 4 miles from the entrance to the Monument, you will enter Rincon Valley (elev. 2906'). Who knows what this will look like when you read this book, as this area has been the focus of a zoning dispute since the mid-1980s. Rocking K Ranch may or may not become a satellite town of Tucson, depending upon who wins the war. At this writing Rincon Valley consists of a delightful stretch of road, a few houses, the friendly people at the Rincon Creek Market, and the much-debated Rocking K. A small cemetery stands on private land .7 miles beyond the store.

Making it a Loop — Most riders stay on Old Spanish Trail and do a simple out-and-back to Colossal Cave, but I much prefer to take a right on Camino Loma Alta (13.1 miles from Broadway and 7.2 from the Monument). A dirt road when Ed Stiles and Mort Solot wrote the original version of this book, Camino Loma Alta (elev. here, 3160') is now a paved shortcut between Vail and east Tucson. Follow it for 3.0 miles until you reach Colossal Cave Road (elev. 3240'). Turn left. *[note: If you are taking Ride Three, The Vail-Corona de Tucson Loop, go right and turn in this book to Ride Three.]*

On to The Cave — The next 4.1 miles feature a slow climb followed by some enjoyable rollercoaster hills, and then one more good climb before you reach the turnoff to the Cave. On a distant hill to the east you'll think your eyes are playing tricks on you, as there appears to be a medieval castle on one of the peaks. On a telescope at Colossal Cave that pointed at the dramatic structure there used to be a sign that succinctly answered the two most-often-asked questions about the building: "Yes, it is, and no, you can't."

The Final Assault — When you reach the turnoff to the Cave (elev. 3520'), 20.2 miles from your Broadway beginning, you'll be facing the steepest climb of the ride, the .4-mile pull to the parking lot (elev. 3680'). This is an excellent test of either your lowest gear (climbing passively) or your aerobic capacity (standing and crunching). *[note: You could, of course, avoid the hill by simply heading back on Old Spanish Trail.]*

Colossal Cave — In the introduction to this book, I suggested that you should read each ride in its entirety before you embark, and here's a good example why: bicycles are not allowed beyond the parking lot, where there is a bike rack, but if you're like me, you're not going to leave your bike in such a public place without a good lock. So, if you want to go down to the restrooms, snack bar, or gift shop, secure your bicycle.

Colossal Cave is well worth visiting, but probably on a non-cycling trip. It's a dry cave with a 40-minute tour that takes you to some beautiful sights. The cave is a constant 72 degrees inside, which may tempt some summer riders into never leaving for the return trip. You do, however, have a delightful downhill ride back.

The Fast Descent — Be careful leaving the Cave's parking lot. You exit to the north of the lot and almost immediately zoom towards the desert floor. But beware of cross traffic at the park's entrance and a cattle guard just beyond it. The 11.4-mile return to Saguaro National Monument will be swift. Do watch out for sand in dips during the rainy season. Your distance for the loop will be 38.3 miles if you didn't ride the Monument.

Other Suggestions — Tucson East

Broadway-Speedway Loop — East Tucson features some fine roads, but many of them become narrow just as they get into beautiful areas. Broadway and Speedway are notable examples. But here's a Sunday morning favorite of mine: Broadway and Swan to the end of Broadway (beyond Freeman Road); return to Freeman, turn north to Speedway, turn right again and proceed to the end of Speedway. Both Broadway and Speedway end with spectacular views of the Rincon Mountains. Then take Speedway back into town. If you leave early enough, you can make this 28-mile ride with little traffic.

Snyder Road and Soldier Trail — The northeasternmost primary roads in Tucson make for delightful riding. The only problem I've found is that making a logical loop using those two roads involves using Bear Canyon Road and Redington Road, which are narrow with no shoulder.

Climbing Mt. Lemmon — Catalina Highway (the Mount Lemmon Road) can be an exhilarating and challenging road when the hoards aren't careening up the mountain. It's also undergoing extensive improvements in the 1990s, and until it's completed I won't ride it again — I have felt too uncomfortable climbing the narrow road knowing that some drivers may not be in prime driving shape. And descending from Mt. Lemmon with narrow tires can be quite hazardous. I know the racers love to train on this road, but the next time I descend I'll have my mountain bike with its bigger tires and beefier brakes. Besides, the real way to climb Mt. Lemmon is the back way by mountain bike. It's the quieter, more spectacular, and more difficult way up (see Chapter Seven, Ride Four).

Tucson South

Ride Three — The Vail-Corona de Tucson Loop (48 miles)

One of the delights of this loop is that it looks so different when you reverse it. In fact, it's almost a new ride.

Tucson to Vail — I'm taking you in a clockwise loop for one simple reason: it'll take fewer words. Here's why: start from Broadway and Old Spanish Trail and follow the directions of Ride One in this chapter to Saguaro National Monument. I wouldn't do the Loop, however, as you're going to get plenty of miles. Then follow Ride Two from the Monument out through Rincon Valley, turn right on Camino Loma Alta, and proceed to Colossal Cave Road (16.1 miles into your loop). There Ride Two goes left to Colossal Cave; your ride turns right to Vail.

You will have been climbing for most of your ride to this point,but you'll have a quick descent to the Pantano Wash, followed by an uphill to Vail (elev. 3323').

Named for ranchers Walter and Edward Vail, this small community (17.5 miles into your loop) came into existence as a rail stop. On your left will be the Shrine of Santa Rita church and on your right an old adobe feed store, now replaced by a newer building behind it.

Continue southeast out of Vail and cross I-10. Chapter Three's Ride Two, The Nogales Overnight, has taken the same route as you

9

to this point, but it turns left on the frontage road before I-10 and heads to Sonoita. You are now on Wentworth Road with its steady climb and little traffic. At Sahuarita Road (23.6 miles from Broadway), turn right, climb a short rise (elev.3600'), and begin a pleasant 3.0-mile downhill to a stop sign.

Corona de Tucson — Corona de Tucson (elev. 3310') has a convenience store up the road to the south, or, if it's a weekend, you might refuel at the American Legion Post 109 hall (turn north at the stop sign; it's down the road on your right), where the group I ride with has eaten breakfast countless times.

Return to Tucson — Continue north for another enjoyable downhill of 5.0 miles to Dawn Road. Here you need to make a choice of routes. The simpler, shorter route is to go straight, cross I-10, and ride on Houghton Road all the way to Old Spanish Trail, a distance of 11.2 miles. Then turn left and return to Broadway for a 45.8-mile loop. I don't recommend it. Houghton has quite a bit of fast traffic and at this writing is a narrow, two-lane road with no appreciable shoulder.

The alternative is much more pleasant. You'll see fewer cars for most of the route and have wide streets when you do join the traffic of Tucson. Turn left on Dawn and ride for 2.9 miles. Along this route, Dawn turns onto Harrison, and Harrison becomes Rocket. You'll have a stop sign at Rita Road and then cross I-10 (elev. 2949'). After you pass the IBM plant, turn left on The Old Vail Road (36.8 miles into the ride). Follow this route for 1.6 miles to Valencia Road, turn left, and continue 2.3 miles to Kolb Road. Turn right and ride 5.8 miles to Broadway. Take another right and return to your car for a total of 48.2 miles. *[note: One other alternative is to ride south from Dawn on Houghton 3.8 miles to the Old Vail Road, turn left, and go 1.9 miles to Rita Road. There you will rejoin the recommended route.]*

Ride Four — The Sahuarita-Corona de Tucson Loop (45 miles)

Made possible when the road was paved between Sahuarita and Corona de Tucson in 1990, this loop (or variants of it) has become an immediate favorite with cyclists.

I started this ride at the corner of Valencia and Kolb (elev. 2787'), and it is from that point that I'll give distances. Ride west on Valencia for 4.3 miles. Turn south on Alvernon, which angles around and becomes the Hughes Access Road. At 10.2 miles you'll come to the Old Nogales Highway. Turn left (south) and ride 9.2 miles to Sahuarita (elev. 2702'). The One-Stop Market stands on the southwest corner (try their fruit-filled empanadas).

Cross the railroad tracks and ride east on Sahuarita Road, which becomes a smooth and steady climb. At 11.0 miles from Sahuarita and 30.4 miles into your ride, you'll arrive at Corona de Tucson (elev. 3310'). From here, follow the directions in Ride Three of this chapter beginning with "Corona de Tucson." You definitely want to return to Tucson via Rita Road and Valencia, since your car sits at Kolb and Valencia.

Other Suggestions — Tucson South

Expanding Loops — Both rides Three and Four can be expanded easily to give extra miles. For example, on Ride Three you could turn left on the frontage road south of Vail, before you cross I-10, and ride east to state route 83, the road to Sonoita. Then turn right on Sahuarita Road and go to Corona de Tucson.

Ride Four can also be expanded, either by riding east to state route 83 instead of south from Corona de Tucson, or by riding to San Xavier Mission and then south on Mission Road. You would then turn south on Helmet Peak-Sahuarita Road and ride east to Sahuarita and then on to Corona de Tucson.

Combining Loops — Instead of turning south at Corona de Tucson on Ride Three, ride west to Sahuarita and then north on the Old Nogales Highway. If you started from Broadway and Old Spanish Trail, this would be a 65-mile ride.

Tucson West

Ride Five — The Gates Pass-Desert Museum Loop (31 miles)

On virtually any pleasant morning you'll find cyclists doing a version of this route. I always start from the Broadway-Swan area, but I'll give mileage starting at Pima College's west campus (elev. 2473'), about 8 miles west of mid-town Tucson, because the actual loop part of this trip begins and ends there. *[**Caution:** this is not a ride for novices, as you have to feel confident about negotiating the narrow roads with the presence of other vehicles.]*

Pima College to Gates Pass — Ride west for 2.8 miles on Anklam, a hilly, narrow road, to Speedway (elev. 2618'). Turn left and begin the uphill but beautiful route to Gates Pass. The road is narrow and frequently has a lot of traffic, so the earlier start the better. If you are riding with others, by all means ride single file. The route gets quite steep on two occasions, but both climbs are short. At the pass itself, 5.5 miles into your ride (elev. 3172'), you'll have a picnic area to your right that is a good place to catch your wind and survey the gorgeous desert into which you are about to descend.

Gates Pass to the Desert Museum — Here is another reason that this is not a novice's ride: the descent from the pass is steep and narrow. It's also incredibly exhilarating, but be careful and stay in control. At the base you'll have even more downhill into open, rolling terrain. When you breeze through this part of the ride, you'll remem-

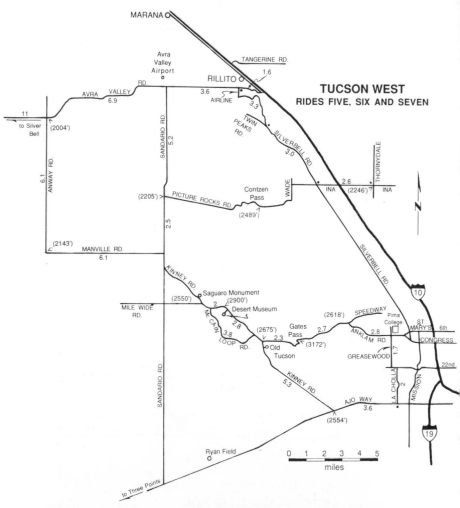

MARANA

Avra
Valley
Airport

TANGERINE RD.
1.6

RILLITO

TUCSON WEST
RIDES FIVE, SIX AND SEVEN

AVRA VALLEY RD.
6.9

3.6
AIRLINE
3.3

TWIN PEAKS RD.

SILVERBELL RD.
3.0

THORNYDALE

11
to Silver
Bell
(2004')

SANDARIO RD.
5.2

ANWAY RD.
6.1

PICTURE ROCKS RD.
(2205') >

Contzen
Pass

WADE

2.6
INA (2246') 7 INA

(2489')

2.5

(2143')
MANVILLE RD.
6.1

SILVERBELL RD.

10

KINNEY RD.

MILE WIDE
RD.

SANDARIO RD.

(2550')
Saguaro Monument
(2900')
2
Desert Museum
2
2.8
3.8
(2675')
2.3
Old
Tucson

MC CAIN LOOP RD.

Gates
Pass
2.7
(3172')

(2618')

SPEEDWAY
Pima
College

ANKLAM RD.
2.8

ST.
MARY'S 6th

CONGRESS

GREASEWOOD

LA CHOLLA

MISSION

22nd

KINNEY RD
5.3

AJO WAY
3.6
(2554')

Ryan Field

0 1 2 3 4 5
miles

19

to Three Points

ber why you bought a bicycle, something you might have questioned
on your climb up to Gates Pass. At 7.8 miles into your ride, you'll
come to Kinney Road (elev. 2675'). You can take the short way back
by turning left and cutting 11 miles off your trip, but turn right for the
better ride, as the scenery only gets more beautiful.

You now have a 2.8-mile climb in some of the best desert terrain
west Tucson has to offer. The Arizona-Sonora Desert Museum is one
of the world's best zoos and also features displays of natural history
and botanical interest. Today, however, is probably not the best time
to visit; take several hours when you don't smell bad and don't have
on funny clothes.

Saguaro Monument West — Just beyond the museum you
top a rise (elev. 2900') and have a delightful, although somewhat
bumpy, descent to Saguaro National Monument West (elev. 2550').

12

Riding from Gates Pass toward Old Tucson

Turn right into the Monument and stop at the visitor center if you want water and a pleasant rest stop at the 12.6-mile mark of your 31-mile journey. You have reached the turnaround spot for this tour, although you can expand it easily by continuing west into Avra Valley via Kinney and Sandario roads (see map).

McCain Loop Road — Instead of returning the way you came, take this marvelous side trip. When you retrace your route and leave the monument, turn left at the stop sign and then go right at the first paved road, McCain Loop Road, which is west Tucson's answer to east Tucson's Saguaro National Monument Loop (see Ride One of this chapter). Although the 3.8-mile route could use repaving, you'll still enjoy ambling through the rolling, spectacular desert terrain that lies behind the Desert Museum. You're likely to see little or no traffic. Proceed to the stop sign at Kinney Road, turn right, and retrace your earlier route for .6 miles to the intersection of Kinney Road and Gates Pass Road, now 20 miles into your ride.

McCain Loop Road

Old Tucson to New Tucson — You could, of course, turn left and climb Gates Pass one more time, but— trust me— it's much tougher climbing the pass from this side. Instead, stay on Kinney Road past Old Tucson for 3.4 miles of pleasant desert riding featuring mountain vistas in all directions. Kinney is a beautiful, curving, rolling road that flattens out as you leave Tucson Mountain Park and come upon commercial development. From there you have 1.9 more miles before arriving at Ajo Way (elev. 2584'). Turn left onto the wide shoulder and ride 3.6 miles to La Cholla Boulevard. Turn left on La Cholla, where you'll find a short, steep hill, and proceed north for 2.0 miles to 22nd Street. Turn left to Greasewood, take a right, and return to Anklam Road and Pima College.

Ride Six — The Picture Rocks-Avra Valley Loop (46 miles)

Northwest Tucson has many natural areas that invite cycling, and Avra Valley has some of the best. This loop takes you over a second Tucson Mountain pass (Gates Pass, in Ride Five, was the first) and out into a spacious valley for a route through farm fields and desert.

The route starts at Ina and Thornydale on Tucson's far northwest side (elev. 2246'). Ride west on Ina past Silverbell Road and turn left on Wade, 4.1 miles into your loop (Ina goes to dirt and ends). Wade begins a winding climb for 1.5 miles up to Contzen Pass (elev. 2489') and becomes Picture Rocks Road, which works its way across the desert to Sandario Road at 11.6 miles into your ride (elev. 2205'). Here you can cut 16.4 miles off the loop by turning right and taking a 5.2-mile slightly downhill jaunt to Avra Valley Road. If you decide to do that, skip to "Back to Tucson," below.

Avra Valley — A northern extension of the Altar Valley (see Ride Eight of this chapter), Avra Valley is known for its fields of cotton and other staples and for its water supply, part of which the city of Tucson taps. For a good look at the valley, turn left (south) on Sandario and ride 2.5 miles to Manville Road, turn right, and begin a delightful, low-traffic downhill for 6.1 miles to Anway Road (elev. 2143'). Turn right again and head north for 6.1 miles to Avra Valley Road (elev. 2004'), where you will find a market on the northeast corner that has sold me cold drinks more than once. You will turn right once again, but you might look down the road to your left, as that is the way to the ghost town of Silver Bell, featured in the next ride in this chapter.

Now 26.3 miles into your loop, head east on Avra Valley Road, which has an adequate shoulder and wide lanes. After 6.8 miles from Anway Road you'll pass the Avra Valley Airport. Its Sky Rider Coffee Shop is a favorite breakfast stop for cyclists.

Back to Tucson — Just beyond the airport, Sandario Road ends at Avra Valley Road. The short cut mentioned earlier rejoins the main loop here. Riders on the short loop will have 16.8 miles at this point; the main loop riders will have 33.2. Continue east on Avra Valley Road for 3.6 miles and turn right on Airline Road. Follow it into — no kidding — Rattlesnake Pass (elev. 2140').

At 40.1 miles into your ride (23.7 on the short loop), take a left as Silverbell Road becomes a wide parkway with a bike lane. In 3.0 miles you'll return to Ina Road. Turn left and retrace your route 2.6 miles to your car for 45.7 miles on the long loop or 29.3 miles on the short one. As you rejoin the turmoil of urban life, make a resolution to escape soon by taking the ride that follows — the ride to Silver Bell. That resolution will make crosstown traffic more bearable.

Ride Seven — Avra Valley to Silver Bell (46 miles)

Silver Bell has been twice a ghost. The first town, spelled Silverbell, stood on the northwest side of the Silverbell Mountains. It was a copper mining town off and on from the 1860s to the 1920s. The second town, spelled Silver Bell, was located on the southwest end of the mountains near a new mine that opened in 1948. But in the 1980s the second town also died as copper prices fell. Silver Bell, which was once a tidy community of homes with such amenities as a baseball park, community center, post office, and the Avra-Bell Market, was uprooted and sold house by house. Since Silver Bell is a ghost town, its road has only ghost cars. It's a dandy for bicyclists.

Avra Valley Road — Park your car at Avra Valley Road and I-10 (exit 242), about 21 miles northwest of midtown Tucson. Proceed west on Avra Valley Road, which crosses the Santa Cruz River in just under a mile from your car. You'll also cross the conveyor belt of a cement company; the belt originates at Twin Peaks, one peak of which is slowly disappearing into cement bags for Tucson curbs, sidewalks, buildings, and patios. As you come out into the open land of Avra Valley (elev. 2067'), you'll be able to see the dumps of the Silver Bell Mine in the distance. At 4.3 miles from your car you'll cross the Central Arizona Project canal that brings Colorado River water to Tucson. At 6.3 miles you'll pass the Avra Valley Airport.

On to Silver Bell — By the time you come to Anway Road (elev. 2004'), just over 12 miles from your car, you will have lost almost all traffic, since now you'll be out of Marana and on your way to Silver Bell, and few folks have reason to head up there. You might look over at the Valley Mart on the corner of Anway Road to see if it's open, as you might want to stop on your way back. The road to Silver Bell will get rougher, and there's only a narrow shoulder, but you should be blissfully alone.

At 15.3 miles you'll pass Pump Station Road, which leads to an El Paso Gas substation. From here the terrain will get gradually steeper and more rolling. Eventually you will be pedaling with the mine waste dumps looming to your right, the same dumps that seemed so far away at the first part of the ride. Finally, you'll take a turn to the northwest for a final, steep, one-mile climb to the mine itself, 23 miles from I-10. This is a great place for a group that has been having fun together to try to tear each other's lungs out on the last uphill dash, because the ride back, of course, will have lots of free— or at least easy— miles.

Silver Bell — The town itself (elev. 2628') is only marginally visible on your left as you head up the road to the mine. You can see foundations, clotheslines, a baseball backstop, and the boarded-up Avra-Bell Market in the distance. The property is posted against trespassing. If you are given permission at the mine office to enter the old town, you can ride the streets and get a good idea of the size of the community. Do watch where you're going, since the roads, naturally, are not maintained, and tire hazards abound.

A terrific mountain bike ride, one of the best desert rides in Southern Arizona, begins in Silver Bell and goes to the ghost town of Sasco. See Chapter Eight, Ride Seven.

Ride Eight — Altar Valley (92, 46, or 48 miles)

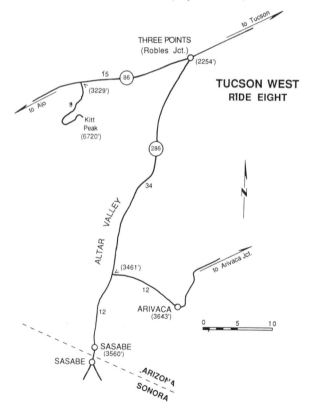

Altar Valley remains one of the better-kept riding secrets in southern Arizona. On my several trips into the area, I've not seen any other cyclists except our group. You'll find beautiful, changing views of Kitt Peak, Baboquivari Peak, and the Sierrita and Cerro Colorado mountains; you can visit two very picturesque towns, Sasabe and Arivaca; and, finally, the traffic is usually rather light.

Variations One and Two —The Altar Valley Near-Century (92 miles) or The One-Way Route (46 miles)

I'm suggesting three variations for riding Altar Valley. The first two start in Robles Junction, also known as Three Points, which is a small town along state route 86 between Tucson and Ajo, about 22 miles southwest of Tucson.

Robles Junction — If you are doing the 92-mile ride, leave your car in Robles Junction (elev. 2554') and head south on state route 286. Variation Two depends upon an angel or two, which is what our group had: they dropped riders in Robles Junction, drove to Sasabe, and then rode north to join us on our southerly ride. The vans ferried riders from Sasabe back to the starting point. An easier version (more downhill than up) would be to drive all the way to Sasabe and ride back to Robles Junction, but that way you would have already seen the terrain from the speeding vehicle, and we wanted to enjoy the scenery first by bike.

Riding Altar Valley — As you leave Robles Junction, in the distance to your right for many miles you will have the pleasant companionship of Kitt Peak, its telescopes catching the morning sun. The Altar (Spanish for "sacred" or "altar") River, which flows south in Mexico, was named in 1693 by Father Kino.This valley of the same name is a northern extension of the valley in which that river flows. The road is adequate with little shoulder, but the terrain is flat enough that you can see and be seen by the occasional motorist. You will be climbing a slight but steady grade for over twenty miles. Eventually you will enter the Buenos Aires Wildlife Refuge, which will extend along your route until you are about to enter Sasabe.

Arivaca Road to Sasabe — At 34 miles into your ride you will come to the turnoff to Arivaca, the only intersection along the route (see Variation Three). The elevation at this point is 3461', over 900 feet higher than Robles Junction. South of the intersection 4.4 miles is the actual entrance into the Buenos Aires preserve. From here you have a slightly more rolling route into the tiny town of Sasabe (elev. 3560'). At this writing a wonderful old general store is open in town, but there are no restaurants. To the south and up a short hill is the border crossing (elev. 3598'), with a U.S. Customs building that was designed by someone who knew the east better than the southwest. You should definitely take the short ride out of town to see it. The Mexican community of Sasabe is down a poor dirt road and is not visible from the crossing.

The return to Robles Junction features more downhill than up, of course, and the last 25 miles will be an absolute pleasure.

Variation Three — Arivaca To Sasabe (48 miles)

If you don't want to ride 92 miles or to ferry a vehicle along the route, a very enjoyable alternative is to start in Arivaca, 64 miles from midtown Tucson. Drive south on I-19 to the Amado turnoff and make two rights. This is Arivaca Junction. Follow the Arivaca Road 23 miles southwest to Arivaca (Ride Four of Chapter Three covers this excellent ride).

Arivaca to State Route 286 — For information on Arivaca (elev. 3643'), consult Chapter Three, Ride Four, beginning, oddly enough, at "Arivaca." At the west end of town, turn right at the "T." The road to the left goes to the ghost town of Ruby; see Chapter Eight for a great mountain bike ride over that route.

On your road bike ride, you will follow some rolling, attractive high desert terrain for the first several miles out of Arivaca, eventually coming out onto the broad plain that is the Altar Valley. You will also enter the Buenos Aires Wildlife Refuge, which will be on either side of you for virtually the rest of the ride. Twelve miles from Arivaca you'll come to state route 286. Turn left.

At this point your elevation will be 3461', or 182 feet lower than Arivaca. Refer now to Variations One and Two, beginning with "Arivaca Road to Sasabe," for the directions for the remainder of your ride. Return to Arivaca the same way you came.

Other Suggestion — Tucson West

Kitt Peak — I'm mentioning Kitt Peak because it's a popular, challenging ride, but I cannot wholeheartedly recommend it for two reasons. For one, I don't like riding on state route 86 (Ajo Way) for any distance at all beyond Ryan Field because at this writing it is a narrow, dangerous road with numerous traffic accidents involving alcohol. For another, despite the fact that the road up Kitt Peak is wider and safer than the Mount Lemmon Road, it nevertheless offers significant dangers, such as sightseeing tourists not paying attention to the road, and natural hazards such as dirt, rocks, and even ice.

If you do decide to do it despite these warnings, I suggest starting from Robles Junction (elev. 2554'). This gives you 15 miles of warm-up time before you begin your climb. The nine-mile road up Kitt Peak starts at 3229' and ends at 6720'. The road is wide, in excellent condition, and of a challenging but not overly steep pitch. The group I rode with stopped several times because of the spectacular vistas. Well, a couple of my stops I only claimed were for scenery ("Hey, isn't that a terrific — gasp, wheeze — look at Baboquivari?").

At the end of the climb, in addition to the huge telescopes, is a visitors' center with numerous fascinating displays. Tours also are available. Call ahead for specifics:

Visitors' Center (620-5350); Tour information (323-9200).

*[**Caution:** Remember that the temperature on top of Kitt Peak is likely to be 15 to 20 degrees cooler than Tucson, and weather conditions can be quite severe there. Also, please use extreme care on the descent. Don't let euphoria overcome prudence.]*

Tucson North

Ride Nine — Sunrise Road and Sabino Canyon
(25 miles)

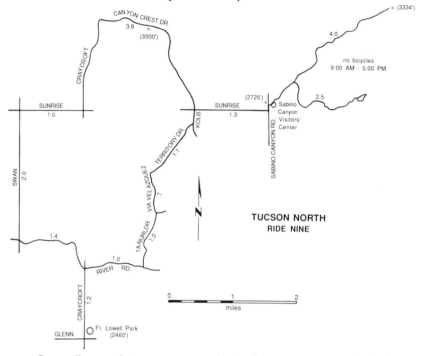

Generally speaking, newer roads in Tucson are more bicycle friendly than older ones, so the foothills of the Catalinas offer the cyclist several excellent places to ride. In addition, lots of riders use these roads, so motorists are more cognizant of them.

Dozens of routes, including all sorts of neighborhoods and side streets, crisscross this region of Tucson, so you should experiment and find your own. But here's a favorite of several of us who need a relatively short, early morning or late afternoon jaunt (the time is determined by when Sabino Canyon is open to bicycles— see below).

Fort Lowell Park — The mileage for this ride starts at historic Fort Lowell (elev. 2460'), just north of Glenn on Craycroft. This is a good meeting spot for a group of riders and offers excellent facilities for post-ride picnics. Ride north on Craycroft 1.2 miles to River Road and turn right. Many riders continue on River to Sabino

19

Avoiding the traffic by taking Tanuri Drive

Canyon Road, but I prefer to stay off that heavily traveled thorough-fare. So here's a quieter, prettier alternative. Take River Road for 1.0 miles and turn left at Tanuri. In .3 miles, follow Tanuri around to the left, through a couple of curves, across a wash, and up to a stop sign where Tanuri ends. Turn left on Via Velazquez, climb a short, easy hill and ride for .7 miles to another stop sign. This is Territory Drive. Turn right and proceed 1.1 miles to Kolb Road. Turn left to Sunrise and go right at the light. In 1.3 miles, turn left at Sabino Canyon Road and right again into the Sabino Canyon parking lot. You have come 6.4 miles from Fort Lowell Park. The elevation at the entrance to Sabino Canyon is 2725', or 265 feet higher than Fort Lowell.

Sabino Canyon — Bicyclists came very close to finding them-selves barred from this wonderful canyon in the early 1980s because of the poor riding habits and thoughtless actions of (I hope) a relative-ly small minority of riders who disobeyed laws and ignored common courtesy. As a result, bicyclists are only allowed in the Canyon before 9 a.m. and after 5 p.m. Please read and heed the speed limit laws and other regulations so that cyclists can continue to ride into this stunning paradise. Like Saguaro National Monument, this rough slice into the Catalina Mountains features an amazing variety of desert plants and creatures. Because you'll be in the canyon when animals are more active than they will be when hoards of people arrive, be on the lookout for deer, rodents, snakes, and other denizens. If rain-fall or snow runoff has been heavy, know also that the nine bridges that cross Sabino Creek often have overspill. Use caution. The four-mile route is entirely uphill after the first bridge, and the last mile is

Early morning riders leaving Sabino Canyon

the most challenging of all. This is a good place to test stamina and/or your lowest gear. At the turnaround at the end of the route, the elevation is 3334', which is 569 feet higher than the parking lot.

Descending the Canyon — Here's an excellent place to show your maturity and geniality as a cyclist. The speed limit is 15 mph, and rangers do issue tickets. Give plenty of warning to hikers, and be wary of people walking five abreast who may suddenly appear as you come around a corner. Take particular care at the bridges. As you head toward the parking lot shortly after the last steep hill that brings you out of the canyon, you'll see a turnoff to Bear Canyon. That 2.5-mile side trip is well worth taking if you have the time. You'll see far fewer people along that route than you saw in the main canyon (mileage for this ride, however, does not include the Bear Canyon side trip). Return to the parking lot (now 14.4 miles into your ride), take a left on Sabino Canyon Road, and go west on Sunrise to Kolb.

Ventana Canyon — Instead of turning left on Kolb and going back the way you came, turn right and climb past the entrance to Loew's Ventana Canyon Resort, 1.3 miles from Kolb and Sunrise. Beyond the resort entrance .6 miles you'll crest the hill (elev. about 3000') and begin an enjoyable descent until you meet one last challenging hill just before you reach Sunrise again. At that point, 19.6 miles on your ride, I suggest you turn right on Sunrise and go to Swan for the simple reason that, at this writing, Craycroft is narrow and has no shoulder, while Swan features an excellent bike lane.

Riding north on Kolb toward Ventana Canyon Resort

Back to Fort Lowell Park — If you avoid Craycroft, you'll ride 1.0 miles west on Sunrise, turn south on Swan, go 2.0 miles to River and turn left. Now proceed 1.4 miles east on River (much safer, though less thrilling, since "Dead Man's Curve" was eliminated) to Craycroft. Turn right and go 1.2 miles back to Fort Lowell Park.

Ride Ten — Rancho Vistoso and Catalina (34 miles)

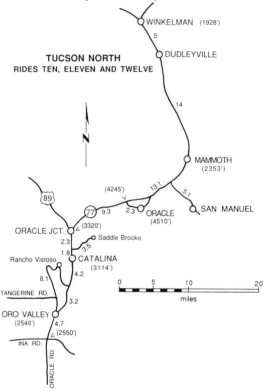

Want to try a route that gets you away from Tucson without consuming all morning? The northwest side of the city is becoming increasingly popular with cyclists because of its wide streets and good bike lanes, and this ride takes advantage of them.

Ina and Oracle — Although you could start at any number of places, I suggest beginning your ride at Ina and Oracle (elev. 2550') because Oracle's extra-wide shoulder makes it deservedly popular with cyclists. Go north for 4.7 miles, passing El Conquistador Resort and dropping down into the bottom lands of Cañada del Oro wash. Turn left at First Avenue (elev. 2546') and continue north when Tangerine Road goes west.

23

Rancho Vistoso's wide bike lanes — and no traffic

Rancho Vistoso — This will take you into Rancho Vistoso, a retirement development that has wide, divided roads and good bike lanes. Furthermore, local traffic should be light. You'll climb up several gentle hills as you follow the gracefully curving road until, at 10.5 miles into your ride, you peak at about 3000' and come to the commercial hub of the community. Then you'll enjoy a smooth descent to Oracle Road (U.S. 89), at 12.8 miles on your route.

On to Catalina — You could go right and return the 7.9 miles to your car for a short loop, but I recommend turning left and proceeding 4.2 miles to Catalina (elev. 3114'), where our group usually stops at Claire's Cafe for a good breakfast.

[note: If you want about 11 additional miles, ride north for 1.8 miles to the development of Saddle Brooke and take a right for a 3.5-mile ride in a lovely area. Then return to Catalina.]

Back to Ina and Oracle — The ride back could be taken two ways: the short route stays on U.S. 89 back to Ina and Oracle, a distance of 12.1 miles. But more attractive is a reprise of the delightful ride through Rancho Vistoso, and that's the route our Saturday morning ride group takes. If you take the short way back, your total distance will be about 29 miles. If you retrace your route through Rancho Vistoso, you will have ridden approximately 34 miles.

Ride Eleven — Tucson to Oracle (56 miles)

You are suffering from the summer's heat and want to find someplace a bit more bearable, if only for a few hours. Welcome to the Oracle Ride, a cool spritzer in the July of Desert Life.

Oracle and Ina — Like Ride Ten, this 56-mile trip begins at Ina and Oracle roads (elev. 2550') in northwest Tucson. Ride north along Oracle (U.S. 89) as it leaves Tucson, drops into the Cañada del Oro Wash bottom land, passes Catalina State Park, and rises to the town of Catalina (elev. 3114'). Continue north to Oracle Junction (elev. 3320'), 16.2 miles from Ina and Oracle. You will bear to the right, leaving U.S. 89 and joining state route 77. The left turn heads to Florence (see Chapter Two, Ride Two, The Florence Century).

Oracle Junction to Oracle — Not long after you leave Oracle Junction, the road to Oracle widens and provides an excellent bike lane. The 9.3-mile route is entirely uphill, but you can find solace in how wonderful the return trip will feel.

Oracle — At 25.5 miles from the beginning of your ride, you'll come to the turnoff (elev. 4245') to Oracle, as the highway bypasses the central part of town. From here you have, alas, 2.3 more uphill miles. The cool and clean air, however, should ameliorate your suffering somewhat. For many cyclists, this is a breakfast ride, and restaurants and convenience stores stand along the route from the highway junction to the center of town to accommodate you.

Oracle (elev. 4510'), founded in about 1882 and named by Albert Weldon for the ship that had brought him around the Horn in 1875, is a delightful turnaround spot for a ride, because from here to the bottom of Cañada del Oro Wash it's 99% downhill.

Ride Twelve — Catalina to Mammoth or Winkelman (53 or 91 miles)

This variation on Ride Eleven takes you beyond Oracle and down into the lowlands of the San Pedro River. As its turnaround point is lower in altitude than Tucson, this is not a ride to escape the desert heat, as is Ride Eleven. But this is an enjoyable journey with one long, challenging climb.

Catalina to Oracle — Drive to Catalina (elev. 3114'), 12 miles north of Ina and Oracle roads in northwest Tucson. Ride 4.1 miles north on U.S. 89 to Oracle Junction (elev. 3320') and follow state route 77 for 9.3 miles to the turnoff to Oracle (elev. 4245').

Oracle to Mammoth — Instead of going into Oracle, continue your highway climb until it peaks (elev. 4440') just 2.6 miles beyond the turnoff to Oracle and begins a 10.5-mile descent (one of the better downhills in all of southern Arizona) into Mammoth. Along the way you'll pass, at 21.4 miles into your ride, the turnoff to San Manuel, a copper mining town founded in 1953. You will continue to drop down into the valley of the San Pedro River until you reach the town of Mammoth (elev. 2353') at 26.5 miles from Catalina.

Mammoth — Named for the nearby Mammoth Mine in the 1870s, the town was the mill site for the Mammoth and other nearby mines because of its readily available supply of San Pedro River water. The main street is east of the highway and is worth a tour. Convenience stores and restaurants are available, but if you're going to turn around here, consider a light snack, as you have a 10.5-mile, 2087-foot climb ahead of you as soon as you leave town.

Winkelman Option — If, however, you'd like to stretch this 53-mile tour by 38 miles, you can head north from Mammoth to Winkelman. The 19-mile route is fairly flat, with an overall altitude loss of less than 400 feet. You'll be tracing the San Pedro River's route to the Gila River. You'll cross the San Pedro shortly after you leave Mammoth and it will appear to wander off, but it's only just out of sight to your west for the ride to Winkelman.

Winkelman — You'll cross the Gila just as you enter Winkelman (elev. 1928'). Turn left at the intersection to enter city center. The town grew near a branch line of the Phoenix and Eastern Railroad and was named for rancher Peter Winkelman, near whose ranch the railroad passed. A post office was established in 1904.

Back to Catalina — Your return route from Mammoth (or Winkelman) will be mainly uphill until you have passed the eastern turnoff to Oracle. But after you finish the hillclimb (11 miles from Mammoth or 30 from Winkelman — and 16 miles from your car), you will have one of the best downhill finishes in this book, as the vistas feature the Santa Catalina Mountains to your left, the Tortolitas ahead, and even a glimpse of Picacho Peak to the northwest.

Enjoying the solitude on the back roads of Southern Arizona

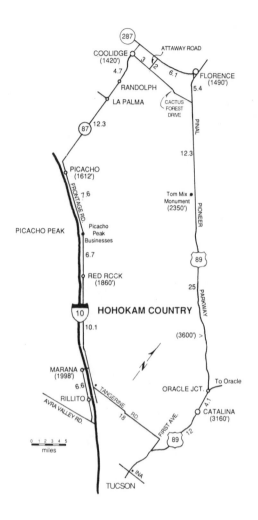

287

COOLIDGE
(1420')

ATTAWAY ROAD

4.7

3 .2

6.1

FLORENCE
(1490')

RANDOLPH

5.4

LA PALMA

CACTUS
FOREST
DRIVE

87 12.3

PINAL

PICACHO
(1612')

12.3

FRONTAGE RD.

7.6

Tom Mix
Monument
(2350')

PICACHO PEAK

Picacho
Peak
Businesses

PIONEER

6.7

89

RED ROCK
(1860')

25

10

HOHOKAM COUNTRY

PARKWAY

10.1

(3600') >

MARANA
(1998')

6.6

TANGERINE RD.

RILLITO

ORACLE JCT.

To Oracle

AVRA VALLEY RD.

1.8

4.1

CATALINA
(3160')

0 1 2 3 4 5
miles

FIRST AVE.

89

.2

INA

TUCSON

CHAPTER TWO
Hohokam Country

A century ride (a ride of 100 or more miles) can be a relative breeze or a merciless killer, or something in between. In this chapter, both main rides are centuries, and a third ride shows you how to combine them into a two-day ride. The first is the easiest century in Southern Arizona; the second is one of the prettiest, but it's more difficult. One ride turns around in Coolidge and the other in Florence, two towns that many Interstate Arizonans have never seen, although Coolidge has some pleasant places to visit, and Florence is a town of considerable charm.

Ride One — The Coolidge Century

A century is never without challenge, because, after all, you have to spend a lot of time in the saddle. But this century has a slight elevation change (only 657'), lots of flat stretches, and the possibility of very favorable winds. It is not, however, a particularly beautiful ride, although attractive views of mountains are ever-present.

Rillito and Marana — Leave your car at Avra Valley Road (exit 242) and I-10, about 21 miles from midtown Tucson. We've parked in the dirt areas near the intersection of the west frontage road and Avra Valley Road many times without incident. This is also the point of origin for the ride to Silver Bell (see Chapter One, Ride Seven). Your beginning altitude is 2077'.

Ride north along the west frontage road; in under a mile you'll make a fairly rough crossing of some railroad tracks (be sure to remember them on the way back: wouldn't it be awful to crash on mile 99?). You'll ride through the small community of Rillito and head toward Marana (elev. 1998'). You'll pass Marana's junior high school and an elementary school at 5.8 miles, and at 6.6 miles you'll come to a stop sign. Turn right, go under I-10, and turn left onto the east frontage road. You'll be on this road for over 25 miles; it's occasionally bumpy, as there seems to be little effort to maintain the pavement, and at times you'll find sand in dips as you cross washes, but traffic is very light. As you ride north, Picacho Peak and the Picacho Mountains will be in front of you, with the north end of the Tortolitas to your right, and the Silverbell Mountains to the west.

Red Rock and Picacho Peak — At 16.7 miles into your ride you'll climb the Red Rock overpass, one of only two "hills" that exist on the Coolidge Century, both of them manmade. Red Rock (elev. 1860') was a stop along the Southern Pacific and the junction point of that railroad and the Arizona Southern line, which extended from Red Rock to the smelter town of Sasco and on to the old mining town of Silverbell. For an excellent mountain bike ride around the area, see Chapter Eight, Ride Seven.

Picacho Peak

At 23.4 miles you'll come to Picacho Peak Road, which heads under I-10 and goes up to some businesses and Picacho Peak State Park. On your side of the interstate you'll find a Dairy Queen and a couple of other buildings, including the ruins of a World War I museum that died a few years back. It's incredible what pedestrian stuff stands near such a beautiful mountain. Ed Stiles, in the first edition of this book, put it perfectly, calling it "prefabricated America run amok."

Picacho Peak (a clever Spanish-English redundancy, "Peak Peak") was the site of the only Civil War action in Arizona: a band of Confederate soldiers turned back a 12-man Union troop in April of 1862. Three union soldiers were killed and three more wounded, while two Confederates were wounded and three taken prisoner.

On to Picacho — The frontage road continues on to the town of Picacho. On your right, at the base of the Picacho Mountains, flows Colorado River water along the Central Arizona Project.

[True Story To Embarrass Mort Solot: Mort was riding this frontage road on the way to a meeting in Casa Grande because he likes to show up at important business appointments in sweaty jer-

30

seys, funny black pants, and shoes that go "clack-clack" on tile floors. Anyway, Mort was late to the meeting and was passed on this stretch of the frontage road by a road grader. No doubt it was a <u>supercharged</u> road grader. Mort, in a burst of energy, jumped in behind the grader and drafted it for miles. Please picture a cyclist, riding a 23-pound model of efficiency, drafting a giant yellow construction machine lumbering down the road. He confided this story to me with the absolute assurance that I would never tell another soul. My secret is safe with you, Mort.]

Falsefront store in Picacho

You'll enter Picacho (elev. 1612') at about 31 miles into your century. On your left after 31.3 miles is the Picacho Market, your last major snack stop before Coolidge. Across the street stands a photo opportunity, an old falsefront store with adjacent saguaros.

Picacho to Coolidge —
At 32.1 miles you'll come to a stop sign and turn right, and in another half mile you'll come to the second "major climb" of the century, the overpass above the Southern Pacific Railroad. You are now on state route 87, which is an amazingly straight shot to Coolidge. It's a smooth road with a generous shoulder, and very little traffic to boot. As you head due north, a conical mountain will come into view dead ahead: that pyramid tells you where Coolidge lies. The vegetation here is in marked contrast to the other century of this chapter. Remember the people Back East who have never seen the desert and who smile wanly when you describe its beauty? This is what they picture as they try to humor you.

The tiny town of La Palma (elev. 1469') stands at 43.3 miles into your century, and the best I can say is that it is Truth in Advertising: *Hay palmas aqui.* Just over a mile beyond La Palma is a large recycling plant on your right, where old Schwinn Varsitys are melted down and given new life as anvils. Then you'll see the Arizona Training Center on your left, followed by the town of Randolph.

Randolph — This is an interesting place. Named in honor of Col. Epes Randolph, vice president and general manager of the Southern Pacific Railroad, Randolph received its post office in 1925. Originally a largely African-American community, the town has honored people significant in Black history by naming streets for them, such as Carmichael, Malcolm X, King, and Kennedy.

Coolidge — You'll enter Coolidge (elev. 1420') at 48 miles into your ride. Named for then-President Calvin Coolidge, whose authorization of the dam that bears his name opened new areas for irrigation in central Arizona, Coolidge received its post office in 1926. The halfway turnaround point occurs very near the stoplight at Coolidge Avenue, where a convenience store stands on the northeast corner, filled with all the things you want but shouldn't eat. We also have had a good breakfast at Frog's Family Restaurant, across the street just up the block. There's also a pleasant park in town: go to Central, turn right, and soon you'll see a gazebo on your left.

Return to your car — Naturally, you'll be going gradually uphill on the return route, but often the winds at mid-day begin to turn north to south. On two occasions that we've done this ride, we actually had a tail wind both ways. May you be as fortunate.

[Personal Note: Mort and I rode this ride, starting in Tucson, on his 65th birthday. On this occasion he drafted me rather than a road grader: you are allowed to draft on your birthday. We parted company in Coolidge, where I returned to Tucson and Mort went on to Scottsdale. When the porter at Mountain Shadows Resort asked him about his luggage, Mort said, "I'm riding it." What a class act! That was a 130-mile journey, something I hope I can do when I hit 65.]

Ride Two — The Florence Century

Known to members of the Greater Arizona Bicycling Association as "The Wildflower Century," because the ride can be especially beautiful in March or April, this 100-miler starts in Catalina, 24 miles northwest of midtown Tucson. It turns around in Florence, a town familiar to many only for its prison, but I think of it as central Arizona's most charming town. In between is some of the state's prettiest and most varied high desert country, which is showcased along your route in a stretch called the Pinal Pioneer Parkway.

Catalina — Leave your car in Catalina (elev. 3160'), north of Tucson on U.S. 89. You'll have a wide shoulder for 4.1 miles as you go north to Oracle Junction. Then turn left and enter the Pinal Pioneer Parkway. There you'll begin climbing through rolling hills until you reach the highest point in the century at 8.9 miles into your ride (elev. 3600'), right near the power relay station. From there you'll begin a rolling, then smooth descent that is one of the more enjoyable rides in Arizona. But remember, you're going to have to pay for all this downhill on the way back. The shoulder is only fair, but the road is wide and traffic should be light. And if you don't know your desert flora, signs along the route will point out specimens.

At 13.4 miles you'll pass a store on your left, the last business for 28 miles (and that will be a restaurant-bar). You might want to remember this spot for the return trip. At 14.6 miles is Park Link Drive, which skirts the northern end of the Tortolita Mountains as it heads over to I-10 near Red Rock.

Tom Mix Monument — You'll cross Tom Mix Wash at 29 miles into your ride and shortly afterwards come to the Tom Mix Monument (elev. 2350'). On October 12, 1940, silent movie cowboy star Tom Mix left Tucson, heading for Florence to see relatives. He stopped in Oracle Junction, played cards and drank some, and 25 miles later drove his stunning yellow Cord through a construction barrier while a highway crew looked on helplessly. The monument shows his riderless horse, Tony, with head bowed. Mix was sixty years old when he died.

Tom Mix Monument

On to Florence — 5.5 miles beyond Tom Mix Wash the Pinal Pioneer Parkway ends, and so, alas, does much of the scenery. The next landmark, at this writing, stands at Cactus Forest Drive (41.3 miles from Catalina)— a four-tier "adobe" tourist attraction (I guess). From there it's a 5.4-mile ride to the Florence turnoff.

At the junction of U.S. 89 and state route 287, turn right to go to Florence (287 goes on to Coolidge). As you enter the outskirts of town, your attention is likely to be focused on the buildings to your right: the state prison. At 48.0 miles you'll come to Butte Street, which forms the northern boundary of the principal prison buildings. Turn left to go into downtown Florence (elev. 1490'). Proceed to the stop light at Butte and Main and turn right.

Tour of Florence — Please give Florence a look. The one-mile tour that follows does not, by any means, cover all the historic buildings of this, the seat of Pinal County, but it should pique your interest enough to want to survey the city more thoroughly. In the process of taking the tour, you'll pass the 50-mile mark of your century.

Founded in 1866 and named after someone's wife, daughter, or sister (depending upon which version of history you choose), Florence became the county seat in 1875. The town emerged as an agricultural center after a diversion dam made a dependable supply of irrigation water available in 1921.

Begin your tour at the traffic signal at Butte and Main. Ride slowly north on Main, where you will see, on your left, a wrought-iron fence. Behind this are the remarkable ruins of the 1884 two-story adobe-Victorian home of William Clark, mining engineer for the

33

James Garner's drugstore

Silver King Mine. Continue riding until you see Gibbey's La Fiesta Restaurant. Directly across the street to the west is a yellow brick building used as James Garner's pharmacy in the 1985 movie *Murphy's Romance,* filmed in Florence.

Continue north to Ruggles. At the northwest corner stands the oldest courthouse in Florence, built in 1877; it is now called McFarland Historical Park State Museum in honor of Ernest McFarland, former governor, senator, and justice of the Arizona State Supreme Court. Now ride east on Ruggles to Church. On the northwest corner is the Michea House-Lone Star General Store, built in 1878. Head south on Church and turn right onto University. On your left will be La Capilla de Gila, the first Catholic Church in Central Arizona, built in 1870. Next door stands the Assumption Catholic Church.

The Pinal County Courthouse

Turn left on Pinal. On the southwest corner is the Jacob Suter house, an 1888 adobe with 20-inch thick walls, which now serves as the Pinal County Visitor Center. The narrow, two-story brick Chamber of Commerce building is adjacent to the northwest.

Ride south on Pinal. On the left is the wonderful 1891 Victorian-style Pinal County Courthouse, featuring its decorative, non-functional clock tower with its painted faces showing the time to be an eternal 11:45. Continue south to Butte, and your short tour is complete.

Returning to Catalina — Remember that you will be climbing over 2100 feet on the return trip, so be sure to fill water bottles and have snacks along. Instead of leaving Florence the way you came in, go right on Butte to the signal and turn left on Main. By this route you can see, on your way out of town, Florence High school with its attractive arched portico. You will shortly come to state route 287. Take a left; you'll soon rejoin U.S. 89.

At several places along the Pinal Pioneer Parkway are picnic tables that you zoomed by on the way to Florence; now they'll seem much more inviting as you climb steadily for almost 40 miles. But after you top out at the power station, less than 9 miles from your car, you'll have an enjoyable cool-down jaunt into Catalina.

Ride Three — The Hohokam Loop (111 or 139 miles)

The Hohokam Loop connects Rides One and Two into a 111- or 139-mile, two-day ride. You could do this in either direction, of course, but the less strenuous way would be to take Ride Two (The Florence Century), spend the night in Florence, connect with the return version of Ride One (The Coolidge Century) the following morning, and ride back to Tucson.

Day One

Tucson to Florence — Rides One and Two do not begin at the same place; I recommend that a friend, who has learned to tolerate your cycling disease, drop you in Catalina on Day One and pick you up on Day Two near Rillito at Avra Valley Road and I-

The courthouse clock tower

10. If you don't have anyone who can do that, leave your car at Ina and Oracle in northwest Tucson. Ride north 12 miles to the town of Catalina and follow Ride Two (The Florence Century) for a first-day ride of 62 miles, much of it downhill.

Day Two

Florence to Coolidge (11 miles) — Three routes can get you from Florence to Coolidge. Option One: ride south on U.S. 89 to Cactus Forest Drive, turn right at the "Stacked Mini-Pueblo," and take this rural road all the way to downtown Coolidge. Option Two: take state route 287 west from Florence and turn south on state route 87. Before you reach Coolidge you will pass by the Casa Grande National Monument, featuring the canopied ruins of a huge adobe structure built by the Hohokam Indians in about 1350.

Option Three: Combine the best of the two rides using The Solot Variation. This one avoids the narrowest parts of 287, features two terrific buildings and a ghost town site, and takes you through some pleasing rural countryside. Here's how it works:

Leaving Florence — From the traffic signal at Main and Butte, head south on Main past Florence High School (on your right) to state route 287. Turn right and head west along the highway, which has an adequate shoulder and not very much traffic.

Adamsville — 4.4 miles from Florence will be the Adamsville Road with an historical marker describing Adamsville, a vanished ghost town of the 1870s. All that remains at this site are a few mounds, which likely were adobe walls, and a cemetery, marked with a large cross. This is State Trust Land: do not trespass. The sign also proclaims that in Adamsville "Shootings and knifings were commonplace, and life was one of the cheapest commodities." It's comforting

Service station without service on Kenilworth Road

to know that somewhere in the state bureaucracy is a sign-writer who is a budding Louis L'Amour.

Attaway Road — 1.7 miles west of Adamsville, turn left on Attaway Road (Naturally, when I found this road at Mort's suggestion, the appropriate response was, "Attaway to go, Mort..."). In 2 miles, turn right on Kenilworth. At this writing an old, dilapidated service station heads inexorably toward the horizontal at the southeast corner of this intersection. It's a gem, and I hope someone props it up. Turn right (west) on Kenilworth, where you will see, in .5 miles, the old Kenilworth Elementary School on your right, a marvelous example of mission-style architecture adapted to Arizona. In the distance behind the school you can see the dramatic Superstition Mountains.

The Kenilworth Elementary School east of Coolidge

Coolidge to Tucson — Follow Kenilworth into Coolidge (the street becomes Coolidge Avenue after it crosses the railroad tracks) until you meet state route 87. Now turn left (south) and follow Ride One (The Coolidge Century) in reverse. Important mileages are:

Coolidge to Picacho	17.0 miles
Picacho to Picacho Peak	7.6 miles
Picacho Peak to Marana	16.8 miles
Marana to Avra Valley Road and I-10	6.6 miles

Tangerine Road — If you are riding all the way back to Ina and Oracle, do not go to Avra Valley Road. Turn left under the interstate at Tangerine Road, south of Marana. You are now 18 miles from your car. Take Tangerine east to the junction of First Avenue and U.S. 89. Then turn right and return to your car. The total mileage for this two-day loop from Ina and Oracle is 139 miles. If you were dropped off in Catalina and picked up near Rillito, you rode about 111 miles.

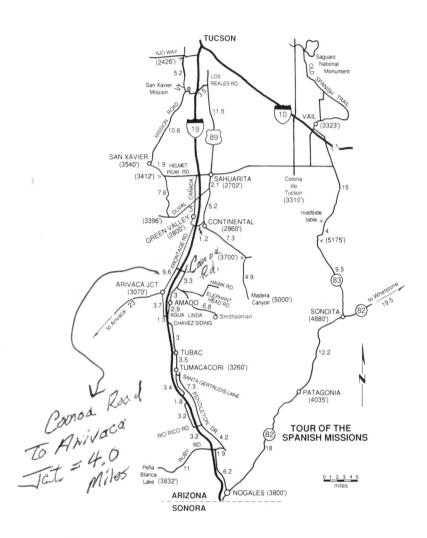

TUCSON

AJO WAY
(2426')

5.2

LOS
REALES RD.

San Xavier
Mission

3.5

11.5

Saguaro
National
Monument

OLD SPANISH TRAIL

MISSION ROAD

10.6

10

VAIL
(3323')

19

89

SAN XAVIER
(3540')

1.9 HELMET
PEAK RD.

(3412') >

SAHUARITA
(2702')
2.1

Corona
de
Tucson
(3310')

15

7.6

5.2

DUVAL

CAÑADA

(3396')

GREEN VALLEY
(2800')

CONTINENTAL
(2860')

1.2

7.3

roadside
table >

4

< (5175')

FRONTAGE RD.

Canoa Rd.

(3700') >

4.9

9.5

83

9.6

3.3

HAWK RD.

to Whetstone
19.5

ARIVACA JCT.
(3070')

3
AMADO
2.9
AGUA LINDA
CHAVEZ SIDING

ELEPHANT
HEAD RD.
6.8

Madera
Canyon (5000')

SONOITA
(4880')

82

3.7

to Arivaca 23

1.5

Smithsonian

3

TUBAC
3.5
TUMACACORI (3260')

12.2

SANTA GERTRUDIS LANE

3.4

7.3

PATAGONIA
(4035')

1.8

PENDLETON DR.

3.2

RIO RICO RD.

3.2
RD.

4.2

82

18

**TOUR OF THE
SPANISH MISSIONS**

RUBY

1.9

Peña
Blanca
Lake (3832')

11

6.2

N

0 1 2 3 4 5
miles

ARIZONA

NOGALES (3800')

SONORA

*Canoa Road
To Arivaca
Jct. = 4.0
Miles*

38

CHAPTER THREE
Tour of the Spanish Missions

You're in Tucson for a limited time and you want to do the best cycling in the shortest time without having to stray far from the city. This is the chapter for you, with its historic missions, out-of-the-way shady lanes, charming small towns, and lightly traveled roads.

Ride One — The Tumacacori Century (104 miles)

This popular annual century, sponsored by the Greater Arizona Bicycling Association (GABA), takes you across some of Southern Arizona's most varied terrain, near mining activity past and present, into a popular retirement community, through several small towns, and to two glorious Spanish missions. Actually, this version of the century varies somewhat from the normal bike club ride, and I'll tell you why along the route.

The ride begins at Mission and Ajo roads, on the southwest side of Tucson, about ten miles from midtown (Broadway and Swan). There are several places to park your car: shopping centers, a public library, and Kennedy Park. Your beginning altitude is 2426'.

You will follow Mission Road south for just over 25 miles, and at the beginning it's a wide parkway with a bike lane. At this writing, that lane dies in just over two miles at Drexel Road. The road narrows considerably, but you will lose most of the traffic in only 3 miles, where San Xavier Road heads off to the left to San Xavier Mission, some .7 miles east. Keep going south on Mission Road, as you will see the church in about 93 miles, near the end of your century.

Tohono O'odom Indian Reservation — Mission Road south of San Xavier Road is narrow and occasionally bumpy with no shoulder to speak of, but the traffic tends to be very light. For several miles you'll be on the Tohono O'odom (formerly Papago) Reservation, established in 1874. Cholla and mesquite will be the most common flora. If you aren't making the time you think you should, it's because you're making a slight but steady climb. As with virtually every desert ride in Southern Arizona, you should be alert for sand in dips; along this road are several places that could have debris.

At about 12.3 miles from the beginning of your ride, you'll cross a private haul road for nearby mines. This is the first evidence of the mining activity that will dominate the scenery for the next several miles. In 3.5 more miles (15.8 miles from ride origin), you will enter the tiny community of San Xavier (elev. 3540'). From here, the ride becomes much more varied in terrain and scenery.

Helmet Peak — About a mile beyond the town, you'll pass Helmet Peak on your left, and just under a mile later, at about 17.7 on your trip odometer, you'll see Helmet Peak-Sahuarita Road heading left (elevation at this intersection: 3412'). The GABA ride usually takes this road down to the flatlands, but I advise continuing on Mission Road. If, however, you are taking Ride 1a, the Sahuarita Loop (46 miles), you will head east on Helmet Peak Road to Sahuarita. But the Tumacacori Century Ride, at least my version of it, continues south on Mission Road. In about 3 miles you'll see the Twin Buttes to your left. As the road heads southwest and tops a hill, you'll get an excellent view of the Sierrita Mountains, with Keystone Peak the highest point. You'll also have your first real glimpse on this ride of a mining operation. On a hot day the settling tanks look like an inviting place to swim. They aren't.

McGee Ranch Road — Two miles later you'll come to McGee Ranch Road, with the small community of McGee six miles to the west. To the left at the same intersection was a road leading to the now-vanished town of Twin Buttes, which was absorbed by the mining operation. From this intersection, you'll have three miles of rolling, more down-than-up fun, with huge tailings dumps on your left, and, at one point, a startling view of the Santa Rita Mountains with what appears to be the Great Salt Lake at their base, but actually you're looking at the giant tailings ponds of area mines.

At 25.3 miles from the ride's origin, you will make a bit of a rough crossing of some railroad tracks and come immediately to the intersection of Mission Road and Duval Mine Road (elevation 3396'). Here you will begin a joyous descent into Green Valley.

La Cañada Drive (Green Valley) — You'll arrive, 4.4 miles later, at La Cañada Drive. Turn right at the stop light (unless you're on Ride 1b, Green Valley Loop) to continue on through the retirement community of Green Valley (elev. 2800') on your way along the Tumacacori Century. Here you will find a convenience store immediately on your left and a bike lane that you will need to share with golf carts (a sign even says so). Continue south on La Cañada until you reach Continental Road, about 33 miles into your ride. Turn left at the light at Continental Road and right again .2 miles later at the west frontage road of I-19.

South from Green Valley — If there is any serious traffic along this frontage road, most of it will turn off in about 2 miles. As you roll along this smooth, flat-to-gently-rolling road, you will have an excellent view of the Santa Rita Mountains to the east-southeast.The higher peak is Mt. Wrightson (9453'); the closer is Mt. Hopkins (8585'), with its MMT (multi-mirror telescope) on top. The large outcropping at the base of the Santa Ritas is Elephant Head.

About 6.5 miles south of Continental Road is an I-19 rest area, but if you want to use it you'll have to climb a wire fence. A bit over two miles beyond that is Halfway Station, which used to be a favorite stop along the Old Nogales Highway, now your frontage road. Halfway Station was an excellent Mexican restaurant, watering hole, dance hall, and unofficial community center. I've had some fine meals here in the 1980s, but it's been shut down, open, and gone again. Who knows what it'll be doing when you pass by.

Arivaca Junction — South of Halfway Station 2.2 miles (and about 43 miles into your century) stands Arivaca Junction (elev. 3070'), with the Amado Plaza, the Cow Palace Restaurant, and a small dried-up lake that also was a favorite stopping point along the old highway. Another building, used for many different purposes over the years, has an entrance framed by an enormous cow's skull that, looming in the headlights of an unsuspecting traveler, probably caused more than one driver to swear off the sauce.

Agua Linda Road — Continue south along this west frontage road for 3.7 miles to Agua Linda Road. Turn left and enter I-19. The shoulder is wide and you won't be on it for long. There are diagonal "tire noise" cuts in the shoulder to wake up dozing motorists, but there is room to proceed single file between the highway and the cuts. The highway is signed in metric, so for just a moment you can feel good about your 17 miles an hour — you're going 27.2 kilometers per hour, and isn't that impressive?

Tubac — You'll exit the interstate after only 1.3 miles at Exit 40, Chavez Siding. Turn left, go under I-19, and turn right. From there it's about 3 miles to historic Tubac. The presidio (fort) of Tubac was founded in 1752 to protect Spaniards living in the area from Indians. Some foundations from that time still exist, along with buildings of later eras. If you haven't been in Tubac before, you might take a short side trip of about 1.5 miles to see the state park museum, the 1885 Old Tubac School, St. Anne's Church, some beautiful private homes, crafts shops, and even the Tubac cemetery, which is located just north of the main plaza on Burruel Street.

Tumacacori Mission — When you leave Tubac and continue south, in about a mile you'll pass through Carmen, a small community named after Mrs. Carmen Zepeda, who homesteaded there in 1918. South of Carmen 2 miles stands the turnaround point for your ride, the beautiful Tumacacori Mission.

"Tumacacori" is derived from a Pima or Papago word and was the name of a village that Father Kino visited in 1691. A mission was erected, but the buildings that remain are of a later era, having been

The Tumacacori Mission

built in the late 1700s. Rumors of hidden treasure caused the mission and grounds to be ransacked repeatedly, so Will C. Barnes, an important Arizona historian, requested that the ruins be protected by having them proclaimed a national monument. It was so authorized by the signature of Theodore Roosevelt in 1908. As with Tubac, if you haven't toured Tumacacori, I definitely recommend it.

This might be the best halfway point of any century in the southwest.The site stands at 3260' feet, or 834 feet above your point of origin, so you have already done the hardest part of the ride; the mission and grounds are shaded and beautiful; you actually are more than half way (you've completed 54 of your 104 miles); and, finally, the prevailing winds here tend to be south to north, so you may even have a tailwind on the return voyage.

Return to Tucson — Retrace your route for 10 miles. Remember to get on I-19 at Chavez Siding and to get off at Agua Linda.

Clever Option — The GABA version of the century returns as you came at Agua Linda Road by turning left and crossing I-19. And you can do that if you like, but here's a variation I like: at Agua Linda, turn right and then left to enter new territory — the east side frontage road. This heads north and will rejoin the main route. This way takes you to Amado (10.2 miles north of the mission), which was established with a store and a post office in 1910 by Manuel H. Amado along the Southern Pacific Railroad branch line that connected Tucson and Nogales. The family had been in the vicinity for much longer than that: La Mina de Amado bore their name in 1857.

Elephant Head Road — North of Amado 3 miles is Elephant Head Road. See Ride Five in this chapter for a wonderful, almost traffic-less tour that takes this route to the east. Cyclists taking mountain bike rides to the top of Mt. Hopkins or along Bull Springs Road (Chapter Eight, Rides Three and Four) also take this route.

Canoa Road — Continuing north from Elephant Head Road, you'll pass an eastern frontage road version of the interstate rest stop that you passed about 30 miles ago. Once again, you'll have to hop the fence to use the facilities. Canoa Road is the first turn after the rest area, at about 71 miles from the beginning of the ride. Turn left, go under the interstate, turn right, and head north to Green Valley.

Continental Road — At 75 miles into your ride (1.5 miles more than that if you toured Tubac) you'll return to Continental Road at the southern fringe of Green Valley. This time turn right, cross the Santa Cruz River, and head north along what used to be the main highway between Tucson and Nogales. You will be on a road with no shoulder but little traffic.

U.S. 89 and Old Nogales Highway — At a point 6.4 miles northeast of Continental Road (81.4 miles on your century) you will come to the junction of your road, called Old Nogales Highway, and U.S. 89. Actually, what is really happening here is that a newer road is connecting with the one you've been on, and from here on in to Tucson you'll be on U.S. 89, the Old Nogales Highway. *[note: If you took Ride 1b, the Green Valley Loop, you rejoin the Tumacacori Century at this point; you will have ridden 32.6 miles to this spot.]* The road now features a good shoulder, but once again horizontal slashes in that shoulder cut down the usable riding area somewhat.

Helmet Peak Road (Town of Sahuarita) — Sahuarita is the spot where Ride 1a, the Sahuarita Loop, rejoins the Tumacacori Century. The town, named for the Sahuarita ("little saguaro") Ranch founded in 1879, features the One-Stop Market, where friends and I have made <u>more</u> than one stop. You are about 83.5 miles into your century. Cyclists of Ride 1a arrive here having gone 24.8 miles.

Now all three rides (One, 1a, and 1b) are heading north to Tucson along the Old Nogales Highway (U.S. 89). This is not the state's most interesting country, but you might enjoy looking at "God's Little Acre," a testament to the variety of what can be called "folk art," north of Sahuarita 7.6 miles on the left (west) side of the highway. Less than a mile beyond that is a convenience store that has served more than a few parched September century riders.

Los Reales Road — You need to be paying attention here. As the highway becomes less rural and more urban in nature, you will be taking a left turn some 95 miles into your century that at this writing is unmarked by a street sign. It's Los Reales Road, and the most visible landmarks are a Papago Bingo Hall and Dillon's Tobacco Barn on the left (west) side of the road. There is some irony that riders on a century of clearing their lungs need a cigarette vendor as a landmark. Be that as it may, turn left on the street just beyond Dillon's and head west. In only .4 miles, so be watching, is the intersection of Los Reales Road and South Sixth Avenue. Turn left into Mission View, a Tohono O'odom subdivision. Very shortly afterwards you'll see the stunning San Xavier Mission clearly in view ahead to the west. You'll go under I-19 after 1.9 miles and arrive at the mission itself 1.3 miles later, at about 98.5 miles into your century.

Mission San Xavier del Bac — There's no other way to say it: this is one of the most wonderful pieces of architecture in the West, perhaps on the continent. Father Kino named this mission for

Mission San Xavier del Bac at dawn

his patron saint, San Francisco Xavier. Incidentally, if you want to reveal your midwestern roots, say "san ZAY-vee-uhr." If you're an Arizonan, you'll know we call it "sahn ha-VEER." The present building is the second mission; the original was about two miles north. Known affectionately as "The White Dove of the Desert," this mission was constructed between 1783 and 1797. Here's a nice piece of folklore: on one scroll you'll see a crouching cat; on the opposite side of the doorway, a rat. A legend says that when the cat catches the rat, it will be the end of the church.

Heading Home — As you leave San Xavier Mission, notice the cemetery on the right. You'll come to Mission Road in .7 miles and turn right. You are back where you were 94 miles ago. Retrace your route to Ajo and Mission Roads, 5.2 miles away. When you arrive, you will have ridden in excess of 104 miles and will have seen, at a pace no motorist can appreciate, some of the most historic territory Arizona has to offer.

Ride 1A — The Sahuarita Loop (46 miles)

This ride of under 50 miles begins with Ride One and follows it until Helmet Peak-Sahuarita Road, about 17.7 miles from the ride's start. Here you will leave the Tumacacori Century and ride east, on a wonderful downhill of 7.1 miles to the junction with U.S. 89 at the town of Sahuarita. You will rejoin Ride One there. That century ride is at 83.5 miles; you will have ridden 24.8 miles. Now go back to Ride One in this chapter and follow the directions in that ride starting at "Helmet Peak Road (Town of Sahuarita)" to San Xavier Mission and back into Tucson. At ride's end, you will have almost 46 miles.

Ride 1B — The Green Valley Loop (55 miles)

Follow the directions for Ride One until La Cañada Drive, about 29.7 miles from Mission Road and Ajo Way. Instead of turning right, as the Tumacacori Century Ride does, go straight, cross over I-19, and continue on this road for 2.9 miles, where you will rejoin Ride One at the junction of U.S. 89 and the Old Nogales Highway (the turnoff to Continental and Madera Canyon). At this point, you will have ridden 32.6 miles; Ride One cyclists will have gone 81.4 miles. Follow the directions from this point on Ride One to return to Tucson. At the end of your ride, you will have ridden just over 55 miles.

Ride Two — The Nogales Overnight (156 miles)

I first took this ride as part of an American Cancer Society fundraiser, and it became so popular with a group of us that we have continued to ride it even after the fundraiser was cancelled. Unless you want to go self-contained, you need a sag vehicle for gear, so we've gone as a group to make the logistics simpler. The first day, from Tucson to Nogales via Sonoita, is about 86 miles. The second day, from Nogales back to Tucson a shorter way, is approximately 70 miles, depending upon your route choice.

Day One — Tucson to Nogales

Leaving Tucson — The ride can start anywhere in Tucson, of course, but our mileage begins at the Broadway-Swan area. The first part of the ride is the same as the first 21 miles of the Colossal Cave Loop (Chapter One, Ride Two), so if you want detailed route information for those miles, consult that ride. I'll just say here that you take Broadway to Old Spanish Trail, ride the bike route to Saguaro National Monument East, continue on Old Spanish Trail through the Rincon Creek-Rocking K Ranch area, and turn right at Camino Loma Alta, 17.9 miles from midtown Tucson. Proceed on Loma Alta until the junction with Colossal Cave Road at 20.9 miles.

Vail — Here you will part from the Colossal Cave Loop Ride of Chapter One and turn right, where you will have an enjoyable downhill across Pantano Wash and a climb up into the small town of Vail (elev. 3323'). Named for brothers Walter and Edward Vail, who gave the Southern Pacific permission to lay track across their ranch, Vail features the Shrine of Santa Rita church and other buildings.

You will leave Vail heading south toward I-10, but before the road crosses over the interstate, turn left on the frontage road (1.4 miles out of Vail, 23.8 miles on your ride). You will pass a steak-house, a saddle repair shop (wonder what they'd do if you brought in a Brooks or an Avocet?), and a winery.

South to Sonoita — As you cross I-10 and enter state route 83, you've come 26.2 miles from midtown Tucson, and you're about to begin a 15-mile rolling climb. The road is smooth with an adequate shoulder and features attractive high desert scenery. Beyond the interstate overpass 12 miles is a roadside table (just before the turnoff at Rosemont Jct.) where we sometimes have lunch, although an alternative is to wait until Sonoita to eat. You have a 3-mile climb after the table to the first summit in the Empire Mountains, followed by a second summit .9 miles later. This is the highest point on your trip at 5175'. From here to Sonoita it's 9.5 miles of rolling, beautiful grassland that has been cattle country for over a hundred years. The Empire Ranch, once owned by the aforementioned Walter Vail, ran as many as 5,000 cattle and was the largest spread in the area.

Sonoita — At the junction of state routes 83 and 82, now 51.8 miles into your ride, is the town of Sonoita, which at 4880' is more than 2300 feet higher than mid-town Tucson. Sonoita was established in 1882 as a stop along the New Mexico and Arizona Railroad, but the area had been populated long before that. Father Kino visited an Indian settlement not far from here in 1698. The name Sonoita comes from a Tohono O'odom word meaning "a place where corn will grow." You'll see the Santa Cruz County Fairgrounds and various stores. Roadside restrooms are just out of town toward Nogales. You'll be turning right and heading southwest.

[note: At Sonoita, Ride 2a turns around and heads back to Tucson, while Ride 2b starts and ends here.]

Here begins one of the best parts of your ride from Tucson to Nogales. It's 12 miles to Patagonia, and the route will be a delightful downhill for virtually the entire route. One pleasant way to enjoy the miles passing along this route is to watch for the roadbed of the old railroad tracks; it will run along to your left, cross the highway, go up into hills nearby, and return and cross again.

At about 5.7 miles out of Sonoita is the magnificent headquarters of the Rail X Ranch up on a hill to your left. And as you enter Patagonia, 6.5 miles later, you'll see on your right, past the high school, a good example of an Arizona territorial home with its pitched roof and large porch.

The Arizona and New Mexico railroad depot at Patagonia

Patagonia — You've come down over 800 feet from Sonoita to reach Patagonia (4035'), some 64 miles into your 86-mile ride. Here you will find several restaurants, a motel, an attractive school on the hill above town, and one of Arizona's very best railroad depots. Patagonia (from a Spanish word for "big paw," named perhaps because of a grizzly reportedly killed near here in 1855) was the terminus for the Arizona and New Mexico Railroad, constructed in 1881-1882 by the Santa Fe. The station was built at around the turn of the century; when the line was abandoned in 1962, the future of the depot was very uncertain. In 1965, the Patagonia-Sonoita Rotary Club began efforts to save the building, and now it houses municipal offices. It is well worth a look.

Patagonia to Nogales — More wonderful country awaits you between Patagonia and Nogales, although you'll have a few good climbs on this stretch. As you leave Patagonia, the cemetery stands on a hill to your left. A road bike can go up the road, but it's rough. The main highway, however, is a treat. Although it's a bit narrow and even bumpy in spots, overall the remaining 18 miles of road are very pleasant. On your right for a time will be the Nature Conservancy's Patagonia Bird Sanctuary, and the highway will follow pretty Sonoita Creek for several miles.

At 3.2 miles out of Patagonia is a turnoff to the right to Salero Road, which crosses the creek and heads north. This a good mountain bike road mentioned in Chapter Eight. A mile later is a small roadside picnic area to your left, and after that you'll begin to do some climbing of rolling hills for 4.3 miles, where you will reach the turnoff to Patagonia Lake atop a mesa. At this point your elevation will be 4200', or 165 feet higher than Patagonia. Shortly afterwards you will be able to see the glimmer of rooftops on the outskirts of Nogales off to the southwest, now about 9.5 miles away. You'll pass the airport and eventually drop down to cross the Santa Cruz River (at 78.4 miles into your ride). Nothing easily won is worth winning, right? So as a final test of your endurance and good humor, from here you have a 2.8-mile climb that varies from rolling to steep. But then it's a cruise into Nogales for the last 1.7 miles.

Nogales — This border town (elev. 3800') is not a cyclist's paradise. The streets are generally narrow, the traffic can be very heavy on the main thoroughfares, and large produce trucks coming across the border from Mexico can make a narrow lane seem tiny, although most of those trucks now skirt the city on I-19. You will enter this world where state route 82, your highway from Patagonia, ends at a junction with U.S. 89, the old main road between Nogales and Tucson. Here you're 83 miles from Tucson via Sonoita and Patagonia.

The border is 1.7 miles to the south. If you have never been there, you're probably going to want to go just to say that you did it, but the streets are not friendly for cyclists. On the route to the border, notice the Sacred Heart Catholic Church on the right. And on your way back, you might want to turn right on Court Street for a good look at the Santa Cruz County Courthouse. If you go down to the border, you will have ridden about 86 miles for the day, depending upon where you stay.

Day Two — Nogales to Tucson

This day should be fun. For one thing, Nogales is over 1300 feet higher than Tucson, so you have a mostly downhill day ahead of you. Secondly, after a day of genuine thigh-burner hills from Vail to Sonoita and Patagonia to Nogales, this day's ride is fairly flat, particularly if you choose the quick way versus the scenic way (more about that later). Finally, though I certainly cannot guarantee it, this route tends to have prevailing south-to-north winds, so you may even have that most fickle companion— a tailwind.

Heading north from Nogales — Since I don't know where you spent the night, I'll start the mileage of the day at the junction of state route 82 and U.S. 89, the spot where yesterday you entered mainstream Nogales traffic. Take U.S. 89 north for 3.6 miles; pay attention at that point, because if you don't, you'll end up on I-19. You're going to take a right on the east frontage road (a rather sharp S turn) to parallel the interstate. Down that frontage road 2.6 miles you'll come to the intersection of the frontage road and Ruby Road. Here it is decision time — Beauty cr Speed.

BEAUTY or SPEED

You get to choose "Speed" only if you promise to take Ride Six, described later in this chapter. If you are traveling through and this is likely to be a one-time trip, you must choose "Beauty," described below. The difference is only 3 miles and about a half an hour.

Option One: BEAUTY

You have made a wise choice. You are going to see the most expensive bike route in Arizona, although it wasn't supposed to be that way. You are going to ride through Rio Rico, a planned community that has had several half-lives and eventually will thrive, for it's in a great place. But for now, Rio Rico is a sparsely settled community with a wonderful road system that does just what we want it to do: it meanders north, going through rolling hills, passing a golf course, traversing river bottom land, and coming out at the wonderful Tumacacori Mission. And you get an extra adventure: you get to ford the Santa Cruz River. How good a ride is this? I've led a group of cycling friends from Atlanta through much of Southern Arizona.To them, this was one of the absolute highlights.

Ruby Road to Pendleton Road — You are now at the intersection of Ruby Road and the east frontage road of I-19. Turn right on Ruby Road, cross the tracks, and climb a short but steep rise. You will then enter Rio Rico. Within the next 2 miles, you will cross a bridge over the Santa Cruz River. If the water is trickling, or flowing pleasantly, as it will be for probably 360 days out of the year, continue on.

If, however, it looks like the muddy Mississippi about to do nasty things to New Orleans, return to Ruby Road and opt for "Speed," which follows. But if the river looks more like your driveway after washing your car, with no mobile homes drifting by, continue on. In just under 2 miles, Ruby Road will end at a "T" with Pendleton Drive. Turn left and continue for 4.2 miles, where Pendleton crosses Rio Rico Drive. Note your mileage here, but keep going north on Pendleton. You'll wind your way past a few houses, approach some cottonwoods along the nearby Santa Cruz River, and experience something perhaps more precious than scenery: silence. At 7.3 miles beyond the intersection of Pendleton and Rio Rico, turn left onto a road (unmarked at this writing) that is Santa Gertrudis Lane. You'll know you're making the correct turn because:

1. You bothered to note your mileage, and here you are;

2. This is the first left turn after Rio Rico Drive that actually looks as if it's going somewhere;

3. You have just come down a short hill and in front of you is another climb — this means you're in the right place;

4. You ignored all this and found out that if you go beyond this point, Pendleton turns to dirt and dead-ends in very short order — and now you're back and paying attention.

Crossing the Santa Cruz — Take Santa Gertrudis Lane, which is dirt but normally quite rideable, across the railroad tracks to the Santa Cruz River. Here you'll probably want to remove your shoes and carry your bike across the water. I almost made it across once on a road bike, but the soaked shoes and the damaged ego weren't worth it.

[*Caution: If the river is running at a speed and depth that is even remotely threatening, do not attempt to cross it. You can always go back to Rio Rico Drive and turn right. You will come out at the interstate. Cross I-19, turn right on the west frontage road, and ride to Peck Canyon Road. Then skip down to the directions under "Speed," below, to "Peck Canyon Road."*]

But this time we'll assume crossing the Santa Cruz is no problem. Get back on your

Crossing the Santa Cruz River

bike and ride .3 miles to the pavement, going under the Santa Gertrudis sign as you return, somewhat reluctantly, to civilization. Turn right and proceed .4 miles to Tumacacori Mission, which you will reach at 20.9 miles into your ride from Nogales. Now skip past Option Two, below, to "Tumacacori Mission."

Option Two: SPEED

You're at Ruby Road and the Frontage Road, and:

1. You have to get back to Tucson as quickly as possible because you have a dripping faucet; or

2. You swear to take Ride Six within the next calendar year; or

3. You have already tried "Beauty" and the Santa Cruz River is cascading bank-to-bank and filled with floating produce trucks from Nogales, so you know you can't cross it on foot.

You now qualify for the "Speed" Route. Enter I-19 by turning left on Ruby Road and immediately taking a right. [*note: I-19 is signed in metric.]* Stay on the shoulder. It has diagonal "tire noise" cuts in the pavement, but there is adequate room for you (and other riders, single file). Exit Rio Rico Road, 3.2 miles after entering I-19; cross over the highway and take the west frontage road.

Peck Canyon Road — Ride 3.2 miles on the west frontage road. Here you will come to Peck Canyon Road, where you must rejoin I-19. But before you do, ride .4 miles north on the dead-end frontage road to see the Calabasas School, which is a delightful amalgam of historic and modern architecture. Remember to turn around after the school and return to the Peck Canyon Road overpass.

Return to the interstate here; you're going to exit in 1.8 miles at Palo Parado Road. There you will take the right (east) frontage road past a unusually large adobe barn on your right; continue on this road to the Tumacacori Mission, 3.4 miles from the Palo Parado exit and 17.8 miles into your ride from Nogales to Tucson.

Tumacacori Mission — Both versions of the Nogales-Tucson ride are back together at the beautiful Tumacacori National Monument. You also have joined Ride One, The Tumacacori Century, as this is its turnaround point. From here on, you need to consult Ride One, starting with "Tumacacori Mission," for detailed instructions back to Tucson. That ride, however, ends up on the southwest side of town, so you will NOT take the turn at Los Reales Road.

Tumacacori to Tucson — Here is a general outline of the directions from the mission to Tucson. As mentioned before, more specific details are convered in the description of Ride One. Mileage is given for the Rio Rico riders who selected "Beauty" over "Speed." Riders who took the short way deduct 3 miles from the totals given.

1. Leave Tumacacori Mission (21 miles from Nogales).

2. Ride north 3.5 miles past Tubac (historic site with a state museum, shops, beautiful old homes, a cemetery).

3. Continue north 3 miles to Chavez Siding, where you must go onto I-19, but only for 1.3 miles.

4. Exit I-19 at Agua Linda Road. Turn left, cross I-19, and take the west frontage road (or see "Clever Option," Ride One).

5. Take the west frontage road for 13.3 miles, all the way to Continental Road at the southern end of Green Valley (42 miles from Nogales via Rio Rico).

6. Turn right on Continental Road. It will eventually join up with U.S. 89, go through the town of Sahuarita, and take you all the way to Valencia Road in Tucson.

Valencia Road to Midtown Tucson — All sorts of possibilities exist from Valencia Road, but here's what our group usually does: turn right on Valencia, turn left on Park, and take it all the way to the University of Arizona.

How long will this day's ride take if the conditions are right? In the late 1980s, a group of us stoked out of Nogales, took the "Speed" route, had a tailwind, worked a paceline, and made it to the University of Arizona in just over three hours, averaging over 20 mph. A group of what Mort calls "Superjocks" finished 'way ahead of us and were lolling about on the mall when we arrived....*Sic transit gloria.*

Ride 2A — The Tucson-Sonoita Century (104 miles)

As century riders know, there are easy centuries and tough ones.This one involves considerable climbing, so it certainly isn't easy. But the last 40 miles can really be a pleasure, since you will have done the bulk of the work in the first 62 miles. In addition, Sonoita is a nice turnaround spot, since it has markets and restaurants. Finally, this might be the century of the prettiest, most varied terrain near Tucson, although lovers of the Florence "Wildflower" Century (see Chapter Two, Ride Two) might take issue with that.

The directions here are simple: follow Ride Two to Sonoita and turn around. You will have more downhill than up on the return route, and after you scale the Empire Mountains on the return trip, you'll have one of the more delightful downhills Southern Arizona has to offer all the way to I-19. Even from there, you'll be dropping more than climbing, with only a couple of short hills — one out of Vail, the other out of Rincon Valley.

Ride 2B — Sonoita-Nogales-Sonoita (25, 37, or 62 miles)

How much do you want to ride in a beautiful setting with excellent roads and little traffic? This is an easily expandable ride that incorporates the best, most enjoyable miles of the first day of Ride Two, The Nogales Overnight. For details, historical notes, and mileage, consult Ride Two starting at "Sonoita."

You may choose three basic distances here: 25, 37, or 62 miles. If you can do 62 miles, start from Sonoita and ride to Nogales and back. You'll start with a 12-mile, mostly downhill ride, have a good 38 miles of hills and flats in between, and end up with a noticeable, but not killing, uphill ride to the finish.

If you would like the hills rather than the flats, leave from Patagonia and ride to Nogales and back (37 miles).

A third option, especially for those of you new to cycling, is to ride from Sonoita to Patagonia and back (25 miles).

In fact, you can vary the distance limitlessly. Mort Solot has a Fourth of July tradition known as Mort's Madness, on which he tests the endurance (and friendship) of selected sufferers of the cycling disease. On one such occasion (1986), he was being kind: the group was merely to ride from Patagonia to Nogales and return in time for the wonderful Patagonia Fourth of July Parade, in which we were an entry. I decided to ride from Sonoita to get some extra miles, and believe it or not, it was cool and rainy on that early July morning. I met up with the rest of the group in Patagonia, we made the ride to Nogales and back, rode in the parade (behind the horses, thank you very much), and it was still so beautiful and cool that I continued to ride the route until I had a century. A hundred miles in July in Southern Arizona? In 1986 it was a breeze.

Ride Three — Sahuarita to Madera Canyon (40 miles)

You could start this ride from Tucson, Sahuarita, or Continental, but I recommend Sahuarita, since it makes for a pleasant distance of about 40 miles, and it starts and ends on the flat for a good warm-up and cool-down. The middle of the ride contains significant climbing.

Sahuarita to Continental — Leave Sahuarita (elev. 2702') at Helmet Peak Road and head south on U.S. 89. Take a left at the Madera Canyon turnoff (2.1 miles from Sahuarita). As the road heads around to the southwest (7.2 miles into your ride), turn left at White House Road and go south to Continental.

On to Madera Canyon — Continental (elev. 2860'), a railroad stop on the Tucson-Nogales line, was named for the Continental Rubber Company, which had purchased part of the Canoa Land Grant in 1914 and grew guayule (a rubber-producer). The rubber company has been gone for over forty years, and now the town consists of orchards and farms, a store (closed and empty when I visited in mid-1991), the community clinic (formerly the school), and some homes. From here you climb onto a desert plateau, passing the new school on your left. You'll have a fine view of the Santa Rita Mountains, into which you will be riding.

At 14.5 miles into your trip (elev. about 3700'), the paved road will veer towards the mountains and become Madera Canyon Road. The main dirt road continues over to Greaterville and state route 83; the lesser one heading north goes to the ghost town of Helvetia.

Madera Canyon Road is narrow and rough with little shoulder, so be more wary than usual about vehicular traffic. Three one-lane bridges in the first mile or so require particular caution. You will be climbing steadily up into the high desert at the base of the mountains, so don't expect to make good time. In about four miles you'll leave the plains and begin your final assault into Madera Canyon.

Madera Canyon — "Madera" is "lumber" in Spanish, and that's what the original attraction was in the 1800s. Theodore Welish built a white house at the mouth of the canyon, causing the area to be known for a time as White House Canyon (and accounting for the name of the road leading into Continental). As you enter the canyon and leave the plains, you'll be at about 4400', or almost 1700 feet higher than Sahuarita. At 19.4 miles into your ride you'll come to the Santa Rita Lodge and Madera Road picnic area (elev. about 5000'). It's much cooler, naturally, than Continental, and shady and quiet (depending upon the number of visitors). It's a wonderful place for relaxing and snacking. This is a welcome turnaround point if you like, although the road does continue up, steeply, for about 1.5 miles past private cabins to a parking area for hiking trails.

Returning to Sahuarita — The exhilarating descent from Madera Canyon will be tempered somewhat by the rough road. Be sure to remain in control, as your vibrating handlebars will keep your attention, although the vistas are terrific — the Santa Catalina Mountains of Tucson, the Sierritas to the west, and, unfortunately, the unsightly tailings dumps of the mines above Green Valley. Remember also the three narrow bridges near the end of this long descent. You'll be able to relax more when you turn west and whisk down into Continental. From there you'll have that nice, flat, and even slightly downhill ride back to Sahuarita.

Ride Four — Arivaca (46 miles)

The ride to Arivaca is a moderately difficult but rewarding 23 miles. Most of the way features rolling hills, some steep climbs, and a narrow shoulder. Despite (or perhaps because of) the challenges, friends and I keep coming back to repeat this ride, for the scenery is delightful, the variety of the terrain is unfailingly interesting, and the return trip is a treat.

Arivaca Junction — Drive south from Tucson on I-19 until exit 30, Arivaca Junction and Amado. Turn right to the small business center of Arivaca Junction (elev. 3070'), about 41 miles from midtown Tucson. Leave your car here.

From Arivaca Junction a short climb brings you out onto a plain. For the first few miles you can see the Sierrita Mountains to the north, the Tumacacoris to the south, and the Cerro Colorados straight ahead. At times you'll even be able to see Kitt Peak and Baboquivari Peak far to the west. You'll then begin the winding, hilly terrain of this gradually rising ride. Be on the lookout for traffic from ahead and behind, as cars can appear suddenly on account of the hills and curves. At 4.5 miles, in rather dense growth on your left, stands a large old adobe residence.

Cerro Colorado — By about 14 miles into your ride, you'll be able to get a good view of the Cerro Colorado Mountains, namesake of the smaller, conical Cerro Colorado ("Red Hill"), just to your right. You will be entering the Cerro Colorado Mining District, founded in the 1850s principally by Charles Poston, although the area had been mined by Spaniards and Mexicans for years before that.

At 14.4 miles is a dirt road marked by the mailbox for the Circle 46 Ranch. That dirt road goes right past the grave of John Poston

(.2 miles from the Arivaca Road). Poston, left in charge of the mine by his brother Charles, was killed by Mexican outlaws who crossed the border on a raid. See Chapter Eight, Ride Six, for a good mountain bike ride that takes this dirt road.

On the main paved road, you'll cross a wash immediately beyond the Circle 46 Ranch mailbox and go up a slight rise. There you can see, on your right, some of the diggings and a small headframe that are remnants of the mining in the Cerro Colorado area. You'll then continue your rolling, curving climb until you reach the highest point in your ride (elev. 3953') 19.6 miles from Arivaca Junction. You're about to have some fun. The next 3.4 miles to Arivaca are mostly downhill with a view into the valley where Arivaca (elev. 3643') nestles. About 2 miles after the high point and 1.5 miles before Arivaca stands the Arivaca Sourdough Bakery with its carbo-load delights.

Arivaca — This is a pleasant turnaround spot for a bike ride. Originally the site of a Pima Indian village, Arivaca was settled as the result of a land grant given to the Ortiz family in 1833; Charles Poston bought the land in 1856 as a part of his Cerro Colorado operations. In later times, Arivaca served as an army post built to watch for possible border incursions by Pancho Villa; General John "Black Jack" Pershing was stationed here. As you enter town, you'll find a general store on your right and a former army barracks (now a beautiful private residence) on your left. The street west of the general store leads north to the cemetery and the former school, now a community center. Ride the area of the town for an enjoyable cool-down. The dirt road heading south from the west end of town is featured in Chapter Eight, Ride Five. The paved road going west from town is featured in Chapter One, Ride Eight, Variation Three.

Back to Arivaca Junction — You'll have a fairly stiff climb out of Arivaca for 3.4 miles, but from then on you should be in cycling heaven because you'll have the magnificent Santa Rita Mountains in the distance to the east as the mostly downhill terrain goes by quickly. And a restaurant and mini-market await you in Arivaca Junction.

I'll always remember this return ride: in March of 1990, as a friend and I crossed the plains just before the end of the ride, I logged my 50,000th bike mile. We even had a tailwind.

Ride Five — Elephant Head Road (45 miles)

Sometimes you need an excuse to try something new. In February of 1986, friend and cyclist Ned Mackey noticed an article in the Tucson papers about the opening of a new bridge down by Amado that would give dependable access over the Santa Cruz River to a small community on a ridge on the east side. What better way to inaugurate a bridge than with a bike? So he and I drove to Sahuarita and took an easy, low-traffic jaunt of just over 45 miles.

Option One: To Hawk Road

Sahuarita to Continental Road (Green Valley) — Leave Sahuarita (elev. 2702') at Helmet Peak Road and head south on U.S. 89. Take a left at the Madera Canyon turnoff (2.1 miles from Sahuarita). As the road heads around to the southwest, 7.2 miles into your ride, White House Road will turn off to your left and head south to the small town of Continental. You can ride in to see the community if you like, but our ride continues on the main road, which shortly crosses the Santa Cruz and enters the southern fringes of Green Valley on Continental Road.

Green Valley to Elephant Head Road — Turn left after you have passed under I-19 on the west frontage road (8.5 miles from Sahuarita) and head south. Turn left at Canoa Road, 4 miles south of Green Valley, and once again go under I-19; turn right, and proceed 3.3 miles to Elephant Head Road (15.8 miles from Sahuarita).

Exploring the Eastern Shores of the Santa Cruz River — Now you have a quick downhill on a beautiful road to the bridge over the Santa Cruz (elev. 3000'). Cross the railroad tracks and begin an ascent to the ridge on the other side. Follow the route up past the turnoff to Mt. Hopkins (see "Option Two," below) and make a left turn onto what is Canoa, which will intersect with Quail Trail. We suggest riding up Quail to its end, just over .5 miles from here, for a wonderful view of Elephant Head (the dramatic outcropping at the base of the Santa Ritas) and Mt. Hopkins, with its multi-mirror telescope perched on top (see Chapter Eight for a mountain bike ride to the summit). Then turn around. Surprise! You'll have a stunning view of Baboquivari and Kitt peaks far to the west, the Sierritas to the northwest, the Cerro Colorados to the southwest, and the Tumacacori Mountains to the south-southwest. Return to Quail Trail and Canoa and turn right.

Hawk Road — Canoa rolls along in a rather bumpy but trafficless fashion to Hawk, the paved road that turns right as Canoa goes to dirt; follow Hawk to its dead end, about 4 miles up the road on a moderate but noticeable climb. You'll pass the closed M&M Market on the right and, later on the left, one of my favorite street names: Livewire Lane. At the end of Hawk (elev. 3160') is a mountain bike-type road leading off toward Elephant Head that I haven't tried yet — but I will. Now retrace your route to Elephant Head and the frontage road of I-19. You will have ridden almost 14 miles on the eastern side of the Santa Cruz (and almost 30 miles on your trip so far).

Elephant Head Road to Sahuarita — Simply retrace your route back to Sahuarita, unless you'd like to take a side trip down to the small town of Amado, three miles to the south. When you return to Sahuarita, you'll have the One-Stop Market for refreshments.

Option Two: The Smithsonian Visitors' Center

In 1991 a road was extended from Elephant Head Road to the new visitors' center at the mouth of Montosa Canyon in the Santa Rita Mountains. The building is base camp for the Multi-Mirror Telescope (MMT) at the top of Mt. Hopkins. The road is extremely smooth and almost without traffic, especially if you ride early in the morning. The climb is significant and almost unrelenting, but it's a wonderful route. The mileage is the same as Option One.

Follow Option One's directions to Elephant Head Road. After you have crossed the Santa Cruz, take the first paved right (1.4 miles from the frontage road turnoff) and begin the 6.8-mile climb to the visitors' center. Even if it is closed, restrooms and water are available just below the entrance. If the view up into Montosa Canyon seems inviting, the dirt road that goes beyond the center is the route for Chapter Eight's challenging ascent of Mt. Hopkins (see Ride Three). For this road bike ride, just return the way you came or consider adding Option One.

Variations — You can, of course, combine the two options for a total of 59 miles. If you decide to do that, you might consider starting from Green Valley rather than Sahuarita, cutting off 17 miles.

Ride Six — Tumacacori to Peña Blanca Lake (51 miles)

Mort Solot and I love this ride. If someone were to ask us for the best half-century in Southern Arizona, this just might be it. You'll have a remarkable variety of scenery, very little traffic, some challenging climbs, a beautiful turnaround spot with a good place to eat, and beauty and good food at the end. In fact, Mort, let's do this one again next weekend.

Tumacacori Mission — Drive I-19 south from Tucson to this 18th century mission (elev. 3260'), now a national monument, which is 50 miles south of Tucson. You can be riding your bike in under an hour from the traffic snarl of town.

Santa Gertrudis Lane — Head south from the mission and turn left in only .4 miles at Santa Gertrudis Lane. Ride down this wonderful unpaved retreat from the city to the Santa Cruz River, where you take off your shoes and carry your bike across the river. *[Caution: The Santa Cruz is usually a very calm, shallow river that anyone from the Midwest would call a stream. Occasionally, it can be very treacherous. Do not attempt to cross at such times.]*

Rio Rico — Shortly after the river you'll cross the tracks of the railroad connecting Tucson and Nogales. At 1.3 miles into your ride, the lane ends and the pavement begins. This is Pendleton Drive in Rio Rico, a commercial venture that has had a shaky past but certainly will eventually have a great future, for it is a lovely place. You will ride a rolling, quiet, low-traffic route that quite honestly is one of Arizona's best places to bike. Stay on Pendleton as it crosses Rio Rico Drive and continue until Pendleton goes straight and Ruby Road turns right, at 12.8 miles into your ride. Take Ruby Road.

Ruby Road — In 2.1 miles you'll leave Rio Rico and cross I-19, where Ruby Road also becomes state route 289, the road to Peña Blanca Lake. The route is hilly at first, then reasonably flat, and then hilly again. Overall, it's definitely up to the lake, a gain of about 500 feet from I-19. The road itself is a bit rough, a mite narrow, and has no shoulder, but it also tends to have fairly light traffic until late in the afternoon on weekends. If you start this ride reasonably early in the day, you shouldn't see too many cars. You'll climb a few good steep hills, but they're short. The last one tops a rise (elev. 4072') at 9.2 miles from I-19 and gives you a look at a portion of the lake. Then you'll descend to a "T" at milepost 10, turn right, and ride .8 miles to the lake's store-restaurant-lounge at the end of the pavement, 25.4 miles from the Tumacacori Mission. *[note: a left turn at the "T" takes you onto the dirt for Chapter Eight, Ride Five, The Ruby Road.]*

Peña Blanca Lake — Created by a dam constructed in 1957, Peña Blanca (Spanish: "white rock") Lake is a popular 52-acre fishing spot. We have had good meals in the store, and you can eat with the satisfaction that at 3832', you've got lots of downhill ahead. It's also a pleasant place just to sit and watch the water.

Return to Tumacacori — We suggest taking the same route back. You can, however, take a short cut that eliminates Rio Rico if you wish. It is elaborated upon in Ride Two, The Nogales Overnight, on Day Two, under "Speed." But to summarize, here's what you do:

Quick way back to Tumacacori — Return to the interstate the way you came. Then turn left after the overpass and enter I-19, exiting 3.2 miles later at Rio Rico Road. Turn left, cross I-19 and take the west frontage road for 3.2 more miles to Peck Canyon Road. Get back on the interstate for 1.8 miles and exit at Palo Parado Road. Turn right, then left, and take the east frontage road to the Tumacacori Mission, 3.4 miles ahead. If you take the long way back, the ride is 51 miles. It's 3 miles shorter if you go the quick way.

Ride Seven — Sonoita to Whetstone (20 miles)

One of the most popular group tours in Southern Arizona is the Sonoita-to-Bisbee overnight. This ride, from Sonoita to Whetstone, combines with Ride One of Chapter Five to comprise that ride.

You can, however, cycle from Sonoita to Whetstone and return for a simple out-and-back of 39 miles or even combine it with the High Desert Loop ride of Chapter Four (which turns north at Whetstone) or with any ride in this chapter that goes through Sonoita. But it is safe to say that the majority of cyclists traveling this highway are on their way to Bisbee.

It's downhill, almost always with a tailwind, heading east from Sonoita (elev. 4880'). There's no shoulder, but state route 82 has fairly wide lanes and the rolling grasslands have no tall growth at all, so the visibility is excellent: cars can be seen for miles, in contrast to, for example, the ride to Arivaca (Ride Four of this chapter). You'll have a pleasant view of the western face of the Whetstone Mountains, named for the novaculite (a sharpening material) found there.

At just under 8 miles into your ride, at about milepost 40, you'll enter beautiful Rain Valley and begin a long, rolling, gradual descent. This is one of those places where you can truly appreciate the efficiency and grace of a bicycle. I can't imagine any vehicle that could cross this terrain so effortlessly and silently. Remember how much you enjoyed this part when you are on the return trip, toiling uphill, probably with a headwind. But let's not think about that now.

At about milepost 49, which is 17 miles from Sonoita, you'll come through a saddle and clear the Whetstone Mountains, where you'll have an unobstructed view across the San Pedro Valley all the way to the Dragoon Mountains in the distance to the east. To the south are the Huachuca Mountains. In 2.5 miles (or 19.5 miles from Sonoita) you'll arrive at the intersection of your road, state route 82, and state route 90. You are in the community of Whetstone (elev. 4385'), with a store on the northeast corner of the junction and a country market .6 miles south.

HIGH DESERT LOOP
59 MILES

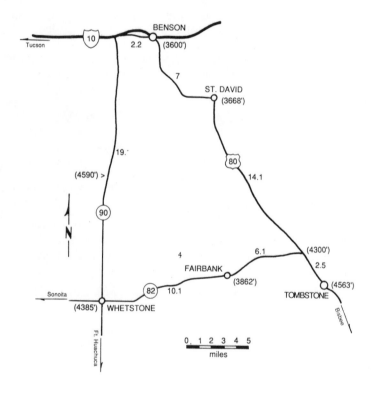

BENSON
(3600')

Tucson

2.2

7

ST. DAVID
(3668')

19.

(4590') >

80

14.1

90

N

4

FAIRBANK
(3862')

6.1

(4300')

2.5

(4563')

Sonoita

82   10.1

TOMBSTONE

(4385')   WHETSTONE

Bisbee

Ft. Huachuca

0 1 2 3 4 5
miles

CHAPTER FOUR
High Desert Loop (59 miles)

Chapter Four is the only one in this book that is not divided into several rides. Although the High Desert Loop does combine naturally with rides from other chapters (such as Chapter Five, Rides One or Three, and Chapter Three, Ride Seven), the loop stands best alone. This chapter features a ghost town, an attractive small community, a railroad town, two beautiful crossings of the San Pedro River, and excellent views of several mountain ranges.

Benson — A loop, of course, can be started anywhere on the route, and I've done this one from three different origins. But the best place to start is Benson: your car will sit in a safe place, there's great food at the end of the ride, and, if you take the loop in the direction recommended, you end with a terrific downhill.

From Tucson, take I-10 east to the Benson turnoff; the trip will take less than an hour. Park your car in the large Safeway shopping center that is on the right at the first traffic light as you enter town. Benson (elev. 3600') was founded in 1880 as a stop along the Southern Pacific Railroad. Named for a close friend of Charles Crocker, president of the line, Benson was then-thriving Tombstone's link to the rest of the country.

As you proceed east through town, you'll see, on your right, several good examples of western commercial falsefront architecture. After you have ridden just under a mile from your car, you'll angle to the right onto U.S. 80 and head southeast.

San Pedro River — The road between Benson and St. David has a wide shoulder and it's only slightly uphill, so you'll be off to an easy start. About 4 miles from Benson you'll pass the road to the Apache Powder Company ("Where Business is Always Booming") and then cross railroad tracks and the San Pedro River, which flows from Mexico and empties into the Gila River— Arizona's original east-west "highway"— near Winkelman. You can make seven crossings of the San Pedro in this book, one in Chapter One, two in this chapter, and four more in the next. Each is beautiful, so be sure to slow down and take a look. The town of St. David, 7 miles into your ride, is just ahead.

St. David — Founded in 1887 by Mormon colonists and named for David W. Patten, a Latter-Day Saint martyred in Missouri in 1838, St. David (elev. 3668') is a bit of Utah in Arizona. It has the tree-lined, clean, wide streets that travelers see often in Mormon settlements in the West. As you leave St. David and head south along U.S. 80, you'll pass some artesian wells that were developed in the first year of the settlement after an earthquake opened up new water sources in the area.

At about 7 miles out of St. David (and 14 miles on your ride), you'll be climbing into some rolling hills. The Whetstone Mountains will be across the valley to the west, the Huachucas to the southwest, and the Dragoons to the east. At 19.3 miles into your ride, you'll crest a hill (elev. 4202') and see the tin roofs of Tombstone glinting in the sun. In just under 2 miles you'll come to the junction of U.S. 80 and state route 82. At this point (elev. 4300') you will turn right, unless you would like to take a 5-mile side trip into the legendary western town of Tombstone (described in Chapter Five, Ride One).

Heading to Fairbank — The road west from U.S. 80 is substantially narrower and has a poor shoulder; auto traffic, however, should be very light. I've ridden these 16 miles and seen fewer than a dozen cars. You'll be descending into the San Pedro River basin for 6.1 delightful miles: You'll be spinning at over 20 mph, and the views across the valley are outstanding, with the Huachucas and the Whetstones spread across your field of vision.

The Fairbank Commercial — to be restored

Fairbank — At 27.2 miles into your ride you'll come to Fairbank (elev. 3862'), a rail stop and stage terminus founded in 1882 to supply Tombstone and the other smaller mining communities in the vicinity. Named for Chicago entrepreneur N. K. Fairbank, who founded the Grand Central Mining Company in Tombstone, Fairbank today is the headquarters for the Bureau of Land Management's San Pedro River Resource Conservation Area. The Fairbank Commercial building, in serious disrepair at this writing, is the largest structure. Two smaller buildings are attached to the mercantile, and four more stand to the north.

On to Whetstone — You'll continue west over the railroad tracks, cross the San Pedro River for the second time today, and climb out of the river basin up the west bank. In just over 3 miles you will come upon flatter terrain, although you'll still be climbing slightly. You'll arrive at the outskirts of the community of Whetstone (elev. 4385') at about 10 miles from Fairbank. At 37.3 miles on the ride from Benson you'll meet the junction of state routes 82 and 90, where you will find a store that sells drinks and snacks, although I've found it closed more than once. A country market stands .6 miles south of here if you need it.

Return to Benson — Turn right onto state route 90 for the last leg of your High Desert Loop. The highway from Sierra Vista to I-10 is much busier than any road you've been riding today, but the shoulder is quite wide and the pavement is excellent. You will now pay for the downhill that will later end your ride. You'll be climbing gently, then steadily, for almost 12 miles, but the vistas will be so good that you should still enjoy yourself. On the left will be the Whetstone Mountains, so named because novaculite, an excellent knife-sharpening material, was found there. To your right will be a magnificent view of the basin that you have been circumnavigating, with the Dragoons providing the backdrop. To the northwest are the Rincon Mountains; to the north-northeast, the Galiuro Mountains.

The highest point in your loop will come about 46.7 miles into the ride (elev. 4590'). From there you'll have some rolling hills for 2.5 miles and then begin a 9.7-mile descent into Benson. At 56.4 miles you'll reach I-10 and turn right onto the interstate. The shoulder is wide but has diagonal "tire noise" cuts in it, so be careful. But you'll only be riding it for 1.1 fast downhill miles, where you will exit for an enjoyable coast to your car. Ready for lunch or a snack? Several of us have planned rides in the area just so we can have lunch or dinner at Ruiz' Mexican Restaurant, just east of where you're parked. You've earned a good carbo load.

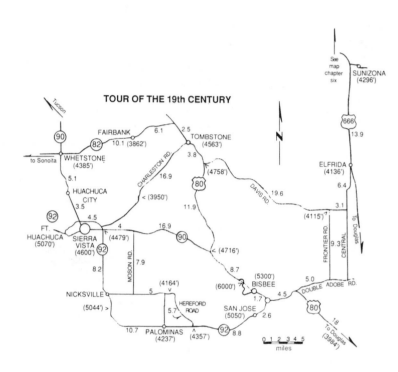

TOUR OF THE 19th CENTURY

See map chapter six

SUNIZONA
(4296')

Tucson

FAIRBANK   6.1   2.5   TOMBSTONE
90   10.1 (3862')   (4563')

82

to Sonoita   WHETSTONE   3.8
             (4385')   (4758')   ELFRIDA
                                                                 (4136')
666   13.9

5.1   16.9   80   DAVIS RD.   19.6   6.4

HUACHUCA   3.1
CITY   3.5   < (3950')   11.9   (4115')

92   FRONTIER RD.
             4.5   4   16.9
FT.   90
HUACHUCA   SIERRA   (4479')   < (4716')   9.3
(5070')   VISTA   CENTRAL
           (4600') 92   8.7   5.0
8.2   MOSON RD.   7.9   (5300')
                                           (6000')   BISBEE   DOUBLE ADOBE RD.
                    5   (4164')   80
NICKSVILLE   HEREFORD   1.7   4.5
(5044') >   5.7   ROAD   SAN JOSE
                                                (5050')   2.6   1.8
           10.7   PALOMINAS   ^   92   To Douglas
                  (4237')   (4357')   8.8   (3984')

0 1 2 3 4 5
miles

CHAPTER FIVE
Tour of the Nineteenth Century

Ghost towns, mining camps, scenes of bloody shootouts, deaths over card games — the stuff of Western legend. This chapter takes you into the heart of Tombstone Territory, providing the cyclist with a glimpse into a famous segment of the history of the West. You'll be able to see much more than the car-bound tourist, as your slower-paced, nineteenth-century-style machine will give you plenty of opportunities to survey hillsides for mine diggings, enjoy peaceful river crossings, visit old cemeteries, and watch the birds of prey circling ominously over you.

Ride One — The Whetstone-Bisbee Loop (93 miles)

A two-day trip with an overnight in Bisbee, this ride is one of the most popular GABA (Greater Arizona Bicycling Association) tours. They start their ride in Sonoita, 19 miles west of Whetstone, and so can you, by beginning with Ride Seven of Chapter Three. The GABA version, however, does give you 19 repeat miles on the second day; this book's alternative has you leave your car in Whetstone and do a loop with no repeat miles.

Day One — The Route to Bisbee (44 miles)

Whetstone to Tombstone — This is the southern leg of the High Desert Loop of Chapter Four, where you will find more complete historical information. Whetstone (elev. 4385') is at the intersection of state routes 82 and 90. I suggest that you do the loop clockwise the first time and ride east on route 82. In about 10 miles you'll cross the San Pedro River, climb a railroad overpass, and come to the ghost town of Fairbank (elev. 3862'), a former rail stop for the mining communities in the vicinity, including Tombstone. It is now the headquarters for the San Pedro River Resource Conservation Area. The best ghost town structure is the Fairbank Commercial, a large, deteriorating adobe on the north side of the road. Six more old buildings complete the site.

From Fairbank you'll have a steady climb out of the San Pedro Basin for 6.1 miles, where your road meets U.S. 80. Turn right for a 2.5-mile ride into Tombstone (elev. 4563').

Tombstone — Perhaps the West's most famous place, "The Town Too Tough To Die" is certainly alive now. During the peak tourist months you'll find more Winnebagos on the streets than there ever were horses. Be extra wary on weekends as you ride your bike among the stampeding herds of out-of-state motorists.

In 1877, prospector Ed Schieffelin saw the promising hills to the northeast and left the safety of Camp (now Fort) Huachuca and headed into Apache territory looking for silver, despite warnings that all he would find would be his tombstone. When he made his first strike, he appropriately named the mine the Tombstone, and thus began one of the most famous sagas of the American West. By 1881 the town of Tombstone, named after the mine, was one of the largest settlements west of the Mississippi River. The prosperity was rather short-lived, as is so often the case in boom camps, and the best years were over by 1886. By 1890 it was a dying, but not dead, town. Its place in Western lore assures that now it never will die.

A Cyclist's Tour of Tombstone — Despite the crowds, Tombstone can be charming if you know where to look. The two

The Tombstone Territorial Courthouse

most famous attractions are Boot Hill Cemetery and the site of the Gunfight at the OK Corral. Boot Hill is on the north end of town on U.S. 80; you'll pass it as you approach the town after you have climbed the last hill. [*note: if you are reading this as a part of Ride Two, The Charleston Road, you will have entered town from the southwest.*] Despite its commercial look, Boot Hill costs nothing.

When you ride into Tombstone on U.S. 80, you will see Fly's Photo Gallery on your right. At that point you are riding over the actual location of the famous Gunfight at the OK Corral. If you go one block north of that site to the intersection of Third and Safford streets, you can see the attractive St. Paul's Episcopal Church, which was constructed in 1881 and is the oldest Protestant church in Arizona. It is usually open for a visit and is well worth a look inside.

Three blocks south of St. Paul's is the best building in Tombstone, the 1882 Territorial Courthouse. A two-story brick building with an attractive tower, it's the most dramatic structure in town. The courthouse contains some excellent exhibits, including lots of memorabilia, an original courtroom, and a gallows. If you were to spend time in only one building in town, you should spend it here.

You should also ride down Allen Street, one block north of the courthouse, for a journey into the 1880s. Several buildings, such as the Bird Cage Saloon, are historically important.

Tombstone to State Route 90 — Leave Tombstone on U.S. 80, heading southeast. On the way out of town you'll pass the turnoff to the ghost towns of Gleeson, Courtland, and Pearce, which are featured towns of Chapter Eight, Ride One. The highway to Bisbee has a wide but bumpy shoulder, and traffic should be moderate unless something special is happening in Bisbee. About 3.8 miles out of Tombstone you'll come to Davis Road; keep on going this time, but note that it is part of an enjoyable loop from Tombstone to Bisbee (see Ride Three in this chapter).

At 5.2 miles out of Tombstone you'll begin a descent into a part of the San Pedro Valley that offers good views across to the Huachuca Mountains to the southwest. About 6.5 miles later, or 11.5 miles from Tombstone, you'll be looking right into the heart of the Mule Mountains, with which you'll become quite acquainted in a few miles.

The junction of U.S. 80 (your road) and state route 90 occurs 15.7 miles from Tombstone (or about 35 miles from Whetstone, depending upon how much you rode around Tombstone). You'll be going straight ahead to Bisbee unless you are reading this section as a part of Ride Two, The Charleston Road, in which case you would turn right and return to Sierra Vista.

Mule Pass — Mule Pass is one of the more challenging climbs in this book. It's only 6.5 miles to the summit, but the ascent of about 1300 feet is steady and stiff. It's also lovely; you'll have good views of the mountains ahead and a canyon to your right. Be ready for possible windy conditions as you come around bends.

Avoiding the Tunnel — This is one of my strongest recommendations in the book: <u>don't take Mule Pass Tunnel</u>. First, it's a fast descent on often slippery, grooved pavement. Second, people just have to honk their horns in there, and if they do it at just the right moment, you might end up with a damp chamois. And finally, there's a better, prettier route anyway. Here's what you do: After you have almost reached the summit of the highway, 5.9 miles from the junction at the base of the climb, turn left onto the old highway that keeps on climbing. I know you'll be strongly tempted to take any route that goes downhill, which the main highway does, but the left turn will give you greater rewards.

For one thing, the climb is only .6 miles and not as steep as what you've already done. And the view from the top of the pass (elev. 6000') is glorious. You can look back over the hill you've just conquered, and, turning around, see the first views of the wonderful town of Bisbee. The route you're about to coast down, <u>cautiously</u>, is the reverse of the killer hill climb for La Vuelta de Bisbee, Arizona's premier stage race. You'll wind 2.2 miles down Tombstone Canyon past some of Bisbee's most picturesque attractions — small houses perched on hillsides, old markets, schools, churches, a boarding-house, businesses, hotels, the old post office — take it slow because there's so much to see. If you had come in through the tunnel and the highway, you'd have missed it all!

Bisbee — This mile-high town is more accustomed to accommodating bicyclists than any other place in Arizona. You will not receive odd stares when you clack in with your cleats and salt-stained jersey—they've seen your type many times before. Several hotels in Bisbee offer pleasant stays. The most well known, certainly, is the Copper Queen Hotel, built in 1902 during the days when Bisbee boasted one of the world's most productive copper mines. My choice is The Bisbee Inn, a rooming house from 1917 that was completely refurbished in the 1980s as a non-smoking bed and breakfast spot. The non-smoking angle should

Bisbee's Pythian Castle

appeal to cyclists, and so should the fact that the inn is owned and managed by John and Joy Timbers, cycling enthusiasts themselves. John is a former national-class rider and the initiating force behind La Vuelta de Bisbee.

Exploring Bisbee — The place to begin any tour of Bisbee is the former Phelps Dodge headquarters, now a mining museum. Inside you'll find interesting memorabilia and informed docents. Available at the Chamber of Commerce are three brochures for walk-

Cyclists on GABA's Sonoita-Bisbee Tour relax in Bisbee

ing tours of Bisbee. You can also have a terrific time exploring on your own. If you really want to prowl around Bisbee, you're better off on a mountain bike because many of the lesser roads are cracked and potholed, and the grades can be really steep with road bike freewheels. This place is Granny Gear City for most of us.

Following La Vuelta's Criterium — This great stage race, held at the end of April, attracts some of the top riders in the nation. The hillclimb, as previously mentioned, begins downtown and climbs through Tombstone Canyon to the top of Mule Pass. If you followed my recommended directions from Tombstone to Bisbee, you've already come down their route. You'll traverse part of the road race stage of La Vuelta when you take the return loop from Bisbee back to Whetstone. But the criterium draws the big crowds. Held on Sunday, this one-mile loop around Bisbee is a spectator's dream: riders tear around corners, bolt past turn-of-the-century landmarks, careen through the business district, and struggle up infamous High School Hill. Following their route (not on race day, of course) at a leisurely pace not only gives you just the faintest hint of what the riders go through, it also takes you around some great back streets of Bisbee.

On Your Marks — If you want to walk the route, you can follow it exactly. But if you want to ride, and that's my suggestion, you'll have to take a slightly modified route, as the criterium twice goes the wrong way on one-way streets. The deviation is not serious, however. Begin at the east end of the museum, which stands in front of the Copper Queen Hotel. The actual route heads south into Brewery Gulch (one way, do not enter), so you have to veer to the right and take the one-way that rejoins the route just past St. Elmo's Bar. Then continue up Brewery Gulch. Take a left at the first turn (Taylor Street), which climbs steeply around City Park, built in 1916 on the grounds of an old cemetery. The criterium takes a right on Clawson Street (one way, do not enter), so you need to follow Taylor to Opera, go past the Gym Club, turn in front of the YWCA, keep to the right, and climb past St. John's Episcopal Church until you reach the old high school, a large three-story building on your left. Here

Struggling up High School Hill

you will rejoin the race route on Clawson, which steams up High School Hill. The hill is so steep that each of the high school's three floors has a door opening to ground level! Consider, after climbing this short but attention-getting monster, that in the actual race the women climb it ten times, the men twenty times....

The route is downhill back to the start. Continue to Tombstone Canyon, take a left, and return to the museum. That's one lap. [*Caution: Remember that when the riders do it, the streets are cleaned and cleared of traffic. They are also better riders than you (well, better than I am, that's for sure) and are more adroit at handling the route. **Do not attempt to go their speeds downhill.**]* Take it easy and enjoy the wonderful, varied architecture that adds to the charm of this enchanting town.

Neighboring Towns — If you have time and energy left over from your rides of the day, drop down to two "suburbs" of Bisbee — Lowell and Warren. Lowell, a one-street business district straight out of the 1930s, is on the southeastern end of the enormous Lavender Pit along the highway leaving town. To get to Warren from Lowell, ride down Lowell's main street to the traffic circle known as The Hub and take the second right (you'll take the first right tomorrow on your return to Whetstone).

You'll cross under a railroad overpass, go past a large headframe and mine buildings on your right, and enter another business district. But the best lies ahead. Turn left on Cole Avenue (the Copper Queen Hospital is on the corner to the left) and ride into Warren's residential section. Here you will see the houses of the mine's managers and other upper-level employees. I suggest just riding up and down streets at random; they're all interesting. The main business district of Warren, with the Phelps Dodge Mercantile, churches, city hall, and a delightful old baseball stadium, is just east of the residences.

Day Two — Back to Whetstone (49 miles)

Leave Bisbee by taking the highway southeast out of town, past the Lavender Pit. If you didn't see Lowell on your tour around Bisbee, take the right at the end of the pit and enter Lowell (the sign says "Lowell Plaza"), which is only 1.7 miles from downtown Bisbee. Follow the main street of Lowell back to the highway. You are now at "The Hub," a traffic circle that takes you to Sierra Vista, Warren, or Douglas. Take the first exit, state route 92 going to Sierra Vista, and head southwest. At 4.3 miles you'll pass the turnoff to Naco, a city that straddles the Mexican border.

On To Hereford — State Route 92 has little traffic, wide lanes, an adequate shoulder, and it becomes a quick downhill out of the foothills of the Mule Mountains down toward the San Pedro River. The Huachuca Mountains (highest point— Miller Peak at 9466') will be ahead to the west, and across the Mexican border the San Jose range will be to your left. You'll climb a railroad overpass and, 13.1 miles into your ride, turn right on the Hereford Road.

The Hereford Road is one of my favorite back roads in this book. You could simply stay on highway 92 and follow it through Palominas, Nicksville, and on into Sierra Vista. But don't. The Hereford route is much prettier, there is less traffic, and the other route will be covered in Ride Five of this chapter, The Sierra Vista-Douglas Overnight. At the junction of state route 92 and the Hereford Road, your elevation is 4357', so you've descended almost a thousand feet in your first 13 miles.

Follow the Hereford Road past some beautiful ranch land, including one ranch that even has a small pond. At 19 miles into your ride you'll come to my favorite San Pedro River crossing at the one-lane Hereford Bridge. Alas, the old bridge is due to be replaced in the near future and may well be gone by the time you read this.

From the San Pedro River (elev. 4164'), you'll take a short, easy climb up to a plateau and head 5 miles to Moson Road, where you'll turn right and have almost 8 miles of rolling high desert riding until you come to state route 90. Turn left and go 4 miles to Sierra Vista.

Sierra Vista — Your first stoplight on this day's ride comes 36 miles from Bisbee at the intersection of Fry Boulevard and the state route 90 and 92 bypass of downtown Sierra Vista. Your elevation at this point is 4479', about 300 feet higher than the river crossing at Hereford. Here you have two choices: either proceed ahead on Fry or take the bypass. Take Fry if you want to see Sierra Vista, to stop for food, or to take Ride 1C, which takes you through Fort Huachuca. If your main objective is simply to get back to your car, turn right on the bypass. Most will likely take this route (A better way to tour the fort is to combine it with Ride Two, The Charleston Road).

Sierra Vista to Whetstone — The bypass skirts the northern fringes of Sierra Vista. You'll pass the Charleston Road almost immediately. *[note: remember to return to this area for Ride Two, a great loop that begins at this intersection.]* You'll have an excellent shoulder for the first 2.9 miles, but it dissolves to make two narrow westbound traffic lanes. Turn right at the traffic light 40.5 miles into your ride and head north on state route 92.

At 44 miles into your ride you'll pass through Huachuca City (take a look at Fort Auto Parts on the left; its yard features some remarkable old cars). Then you'll go down a hill and have one good climb up to high desert flatlands before you arrive at your car in Whetstone, 49 miles from Bisbee. Of course, if you began in Sonoita, you'll take a left turn and have just under 20 miles to go.

Ride 1A — Variations on Day One of the Whetstone-Bisbee Loop

I recommend doing The Whetstone-Bisbee Loop just as described in Ride One for the first time you do it. But for subsequent tours, try some diversity.

Day One, Variation One — Ride from Whetstone to the northwestern end of the 90-92 bypass (8.6 miles), turn left, and go to Charleston Road (12.9 miles from Whetstone). Then take the Charleston Road for 17 miles to Tombstone (see Ride Two in this chapter for details). The original route from Whetstone to Tombstone covers 19 miles. This route will add almost 11 miles, but you'll see some historic country.

Day One, Variation Two — Ride to Sierra Vista as in Variation One, but keep going past the Charleston Road to Fry Boulevard. Turn left (east) and ride 15 miles to the junction of state route 90 and U.S. 80, at the base of Mule Pass. You will have ridden just over 28 miles from your car, whereas the original route, going through Tombstone, is more than six miles farther.

Ride 1B — Variations on Day Two of the Whetstone-Bisbee Loop

Day Two, Variation One — If you just can't pass up descending Mule Pass, you can climb up out of Bisbee (I'd go over the pass instead of through the tunnel), roar down the hill, turn left at the junction of U.S. 80 and state route 90, and return to Whetstone via Sierra Vista and the northern bypass. This shorter return trip covers under 36 miles.

Day Two, Variation Two — Follow the regular route to the Hereford Road turnoff, but instead of turning right, stay on state route 92. You'll cross the San Pedro River at Palominas and start climbing through Miracle Valley as you head straight for the Huachuca Mountains. Continue on highway 92 all the way to Sierra Vista's Fry Boulevard and rejoin Ride One. Or you can take a left on Buffalo Soldier Trail, which has a narrow shoulder that widens into a beautiful bicycle "diamond" lane. This bike route ends at Fry Boulevard at the Main Gate to Fort Huachuca. You can either continue north to Whetstone or add Ride 1C, which enters the fort. The distance for this variation of Day Two is only .2 miles more than the original route. If you add a tour of Fort Huachuca, you'll go 7.2 miles farther.

Ride 1C — Touring Fort Huachuca (9 miles)

Cycling on an army base is different from riding in civilian territory, including a couple of definite plusses: for one, the motorists tend to be very law-abiding and responsible; secondly, most soldiers are physically fit, so they respect what you are doing and may well be cyclists themselves. I have felt both welcome and secure riding around Fort Huachuca, the only active army post remaining in Arizona from the more than 70 that once existed.

Inside this twentieth-century post is a fort of antiquity, and that is the main reason for cycling in. Camp (later Fort) Huachuca was founded in 1877 for the control of renegade Apaches. Its proximity to the border helped cut off a favorite Apache escape route south into the relative safety of Mexico. Soldiers from the fort trailed Geronimo for 3,000 miles and five months before capturing him not far from what is now Douglas in 1886. And in 1916 the post's Tenth Cavalry aided in the punitive expedition into Mexico led by Gen. John J. "Black Jack" Pershing in the unsuccessful attempt to capture Pancho Villa.

The historic area of Fort Huachuca is in Cavalry Park. Stop at the Main Gate visitors' center (elev. 4640'), beyond the western end of Fry Boulevard, to check in and get a map. Follow Squier Avenue into the fort. There's no shoulder, but the two-lane road is one way for much of the route. Soon you'll pass a sign not often found on the road: "Tank Crossing." I recommend giving tanks the right of way.

The uphill route stays on Squier, which joins Winrow Road, until you turn left on Mizner, in front of the community activities building.

Turn right on Henry Circle and follow the brown signs for the museum. At Boyd and Grierson, 4 miles from the Main Gate, you'll be in front of the parade grounds with the museum to your right (elev. 5070'). Visit the museum and ride around the perimeter of the grounds so you can see the old barracks, the gazebo, and Brayton Hall (at the far end of the parade grounds). There you'll have a dramatic view across the San Pedro Valley to the Dragoon Mountains, named for the Third U. S. Cavalry that used to march through them.

You can either return to the Main Gate by taking Winrow Road back out or go out the East Gate and make a loop ride. To get to the East Gate, take Hatfield Street or Smith Avenue to Carter Street. It's downhill all the way. From the East Gate you can either turn south to Fry Boulevard or head east along the 90-92 by pass. The loop from Main Gate to East Gate is 8.7 miles.

Ride Two — The Charleston Road (48 miles)

Perhaps no one can relive the late 1870s, but with this loop you might come about as close as anyone can. You will start near Fort Huachuca, as Ed Schieffelin did in 1877, head for the hills that promised him a silver strike, see the cabin where he spent one night on his trek, and visit Tombstone, the town his discovery made famous. If you really want to get a feel for Schieffelin's route, you can even begin your tour with Ride 1C, the tour of historic Fort Huachuca, which precedes this ride in the chapter.

Sierra Vista and the Charleston Road — Begin your loop just north of Fry Boulevard on the east end of Sierra Vista at the northeast corner of Charleston Road and the state route 90 and 92 bypass (elev. 4460'). You'll be riding northeast toward the Tombstone Hills that looked so promising when Schieffelin left the safety of then-Camp Huachuca and ventured into Apache territory, having been warned that all he would find would be his tombstone.

Most traffic on the road usually dies out in a mile, at the Sierra Vista campus of Cochise College. The road has no shoulder and is a bit bumpy, but the lanes are wide. You'll have a slight but steady downhill to a crossing of the San Pedro River some 7.5 miles into your journey. One thing to notice from this vantage point is how the stark vegetation along the route contrasts with the riparian world that you can see in the distance along the San Pedro.

Charleston and Millville — Just before you cross the San Pedro (elev. 3950' at this point), look north along the banks of the river. Hidden in the brush are the scant ruins of Charleston, a total ghost town that is not readily visible from ground level but is easily spotted from the air. A few adobe walls and faint lines of foundations and streets are all that remain. Charleston was a small, rowdy offshoot of Tombstone in the early 1880s. Because Tombstone did not have enough water to mill its ore, Charleston was founded along the San Pedro for that purpose. Across the river was its sister town of Millville, and you can still see the most prominent remnants, excavations into the side of the hills that were the foundations for the gravity-feed mills that gave the town its name.

Brunckow's Cabin on the Charleston Road

Brunckow's Cabin — Now you will begin the uphill ride to Tombstone. At 1.4 miles beyond the river crossing, or 8.9 miles into your ride, you'll cross a cattleguard. Get off your bike just beyond it and climb the rise on the right shoulder. Across a draw on another hill are the adobe ruins of Brunckow's Cabin, known as "the bloodiest cabin in Arizona's history."

In the late 1850s, more than twenty years before the rich silver discoveries of Tombstone, German engineer and scientist Frederick Brunckow was working a mine here. Mexican bandits killed him and threw his body down his mine shaft. After that, the cabin became a favorite spot for outlaws to rendezvous, since the cabin offered a good lookout in all directions. Ed Schieffelin, hiding from Apaches as he headed towards the hills that would make him famous, spent a night at the cabin.

On to Tombstone — The main reason to do this loop in the direction suggested is to follow Schieffelin's route. A side benefit is that you will now be climbing the Tombstone Hills, and because you'll be going slowly, you'll have plenty of time to examine the area around you. If you look closely, you'll see an astonishing amount of digging and scratching into the hillsides, reminders of the prospectors who were looking to repeat Schieffelin's good fortune. Most motorists would miss this evidence.

75

At 14.4 miles into your ride you'll pass a wonderful old steam boiler that has been placed roadside to mark the entrance to the State of Maine Mine. Just .6 miles beyond that you'll crest a hill and have a good panorama of "The Town Too Tough To Die." In another 1.9 miles, you'll be at the heart of downtown Tombstone (elev. 4563'). See "Tombstone," in Ride One of this chapter, for historical information on the town and consult the same ride for biking suggestions in "A Cyclist's Tour of Tombstone."

Leaving Tombstone — Again, refer to Ride One of this chapter, starting with "Tombstone to State Route 90." This will give you particulars on this 15.7-mile segment of your ride. At that point you'll turn right (west) on state route 90, while Ride One stays on U.S. 80 and climbs Mule Pass on the way to Bisbee.

Back to the San Pedro and Sierra Vista — At this junction you will be at 4716', or 153 feet higher than Tombstone and 256 feet higher than your car in Sierra Vista. Two miles beyond the junction you'll re-enter the San Pedro Valley and see a dramatic display of mountain ranges. Looking to the south and panning west to north you will see the Sierra San Jose (in Mexico), the Huachucas, the Santa Ritas (far to the west), the Whetstones, the Rincons (far to the north), the Tombstone Hills (with a glimpse of the Dragoons behind them), and the Mule Mountains at your back. To make this even more enjoyable, you'll also have a downhill.

At 23.6 miles from Tombstone, over 40 miles into your loop, you'll again cross the San Pedro River. *[note: if you do all the rides in Chapters Four and Five, you'll cross the river six times, and it will become a real friend to look forward to.]* On this crossing are shade trees that arch over the highway at one point. Now begins the final climb of the loop, but you're only 7.7 miles from your car.

Moson Road intersects highway 90 at 26.7 miles from Tombstone. It is at this point that Ride One of this chapter joins your route to head into Sierra Vista. The junction of Fry Boulevard and state routes 90 and 92 occurs at 30.8 miles from Tombstone. Turn right and return to Charleston Road and your car.

Ride 2A — Charleston Road Variation (48 miles)

Take the same route as Ride Two from Sierra Vista to Tombstone via the Charleston Road. But instead of heading south on U.S. 80 in Tombstone, ride north for 2.5 miles to the junction of U.S. 80 and state route 82. Ride west to Fairbank and then to Whetstone (19 miles from Tombstone). For a complete description of this section of your ride, consult Chapter Four, The High Desert Loop, beginning with the section "Heading to Fairbank."

After you reach Whetstone, turn south on state route 90, go through Huachuca City and on to the stoplight at the 90-92 bypass, which is 8.6 miles south of Whetstone. Turn left and return to your car at the Charleston Road.

Ride Three — The Tombstone-Bisbee-Davis Road Loop (68 miles)

A few years ago, this was a ride a road bike couldn't make because Davis Road used to be the official dirt shortcut from Elfrida to Tombstone. Now it's a paved road and one of the best cycling avenues of Southern Arizona— wide and smooth, with little traffic. As a result, the Tombstone-Bisbee loop is an enjoyable reality.

Tombstone to Bisbee — Consult Ride One of this chapter, beginning with "Tombstone to State Route 90." Follow that ride all the way to Bisbee, 24.5 miles from Tombstone. You should also use that ride if you want suggestions for touring Bisbee; then turn again to this ride for the return loop to Tombstone, as Ride One goes to Sierra Vista and Whetstone.

Bisbee to Davis Road — Leave Bisbee (elev. 5300') by taking U.S. 80 south out of town past the Lavender Pit and down to the traffic circle known as "The Hub," 1.7 miles from downtown Bisbee. Follow The Hub around past two of its "spokes" (the first goes to Sierra Vista, the second to Warren), and take the third (U.S. 80) to Douglas. You will be riding between the Mule Mountains on your left and huge waste dumps on your right.

The downhill from Bisbee comes out of the Mule Mountain foothills onto a high desert plain. At 6.2 miles from downtown Bisbee you will turn left onto Double Adobe Road (the main highway goes to Douglas — see Ride Five in this chapter). Double Adobe Road, named for a practically vanished community along its route, features little traffic, a slight downhill, and panoramic vistas. In 5.0 miles, turn left on Frontier Road and head north for 9.3 miles to Davis Road. At this intersection you will have ridden 45 miles on your loop from Tombstone.

[note: If you are on Ride Four, from Bisbee to Cochise, you'll turn right at Davis Road and continue to Elfrida.]

Davis Road to Tombstone — At this point (elev. 4115') you have dropped 1185 feet in 20.5 miles from Bisbee. Now it's time to earn a bit of it back. The route to U.S. 80 winds through high desert country that most Arizonans have never seen, and that's why you'll like it. This is an enjoyable 19.6-mile ride because of the infrequent cars and the solitude that you should find.

The distance from the junction of Davis Road and U.S. 80 (elev. 4758') back to downtown Tombstone is 3.8 miles of mostly downhill riding. Several restaurants in Tombstone stand waiting for your patronage as you celebrate your 68-mile loop.

Ride Four — Bisbee to Cochise (69 miles)

Here's an enjoyable way to join Chapter Five to Chapter Six. This ride also ties together two of the most interesting places to stay in the state— Bisbee and Cochise. It's a pleasant, low-traffic route with much more downhill than uphill, featuring a small farming community and two ghost towns.

For a more complete description of the first 20.5 miles of this ride, refer to Ride Three of this chapter, the Tombstone-Bisbee-Davis Road Loop. Begin at "Bisbee to Davis Road." Then return to this ride when Ride Three reaches "Davis Road to Tombstone."

[Here's a brief summary of that description: Head south from Bisbee on U.S. 80; follow The Hub around to the Douglas exit, and ride to Double Adobe Road (6.2 miles from Bisbee). Turn left. Follow Double Adobe Road for 5.0 miles and turn left on Frontier Road. This will take a 9.3-mile due-north route to Davis Road. Ride Three turns left to Tombstone. You will turn right and head to Elfrida.]

Davis Road to Elfrida — Ride east for 3.1 miles to Central Road and then take a left, heading north 6.4 miles to Elfrida (elev. 4136'). A grateful railroad named this town: G. I. Van Meter allowed a branch-line right-of-way through his land under the condition that the rail-stop along the way be named for his mother. A farming community well known for its fruit orchards, Elfrida, 30 miles into the ride, is where we usually have lunch.

Elfrida to Sunizona — As you leave Elfrida and head north on U.S. 666, you'll pass the Gleeson Road, which leads over to the mountain bike route of Ride One in Chapter Eight. Your 13.9-mile road ride from Elfrida to Sunizona, at the junction of your road and state route 181, goes past several ranches and farms along flat terrain. You'll have good views of the Chiricahua Mountains to the east.

Sunizona to Cochise — State route 181 heads east to Chiricahua National Monument, a place you can visit in Chapter Six, Ride 1a. You, however, will continue north on U.S. 666, which enters some rolling terrain as it bends westward. At 48.8 miles from Bisbee, you'll pass Kansas Settlement Road, which heads north to Willcox through the farming community of Kansas Settlement. Ride One of Chapter Six takes this turnoff. Once again, you stay on U.S. 666.

Pearce — 2.7 miles after Kansas Settlement Road you will come to a dirt road that heads into the ghost town of Pearce. At this point, turn to Chapter Six, Ride Two, and begin with "Pearce." You should consult that ride from here all the way to Cochise.

The pertinent mileage information for your ride from Bisbee is:

Bisbee to Elfrida	30.0 miles
Elfrida to Pearce	22.3 miles
Pearce to Cochise	16.7 miles
Total distance	69.0 miles

Ride Five — The Sierra Vista-Douglas Overnight (107 miles)

Here is a delightful, easy, overnight ride that I took for the first time in 1990 as a participant on a Greater Arizona Bicycling Association (GABA) tour. Known to GABA as "La Independencia Ride," the overnight is ridden in mid-September to help Douglas and its sister town across the Mexican border, Agua Prieta, celebrate Father Hidalgo's declaration of Mexico's independence from Spain on September 16, 1810, an independence actually achieved in 1821.

Day One — Sierra Vista to Douglas (57 miles)

Sierra Vista to Palominas — Leave your car in one of the shopping center parking lots at the intersection of Fry Boulevard and state routes 92 and 90 in Sierra Vista (elev. 4479'). Go south on 92, which has a wide, pleasant shoulder for much of the route. At 8.2 miles you'll pass through the small community of Nicksville and begin to ride along the foothills of the Huachuca Mountains. At 12 miles from Sierra Vista you'll reach a high point (elev. 5044') and have a magnificent view across the San Pedro Valley to the Mule Mountains. As you turn from south to east, you will have an exhilarating downhill into Miracle Valley and the town of Palominas (18.9 miles from Sierra Vista). Just east of Palominas you'll cross the San Pedro River, the southernmost of the six San Pedro bridges you can traverse on the rides in this chapter and Chapter Four.

Palominas to San Jose — Now you have some work to do. From the San Pedro (elev. 4237') you'll be climbing for 12.8 miles to the Bisbee suburb of San Jose. But the road is wide, the shoulder is good, and the views ahead and into Mexico are splendid. The road going south from the main intersection in San Jose (elev. 5050') leads to Naco, on the border between the United States and Mexico.

San Jose to Douglas — You are 31.7 miles into your 57-mile ride. Continue on state route 92 to The Hub, a traffic circle 2.6 miles from San Jose. Here you will take the second "spoke" of the hub and follow U.S. 80 to Douglas. You won't actually see downtown Bisbee today, but you will tomorrow. Now comes some enjoyable riding. For 4.5 miles you will leave the foothills of the Mule Mountains and whisk down onto the plain of the Sulphur Springs Valley. Stay on U.S. 80 for the remaining 18 miles to Douglas. You'll have a slightly downhill grade virtually all of the way, and the highway is smooth and wide. The dominant manmade feature along this route used to be the huge stacks of the Phelps Dodge smelter outside of Douglas, but they were toppled in January of 1991. Some remnants of the smelter still remain on the south side of the road as you near Douglas.

Douglas — Named for Dr. James Stuart Douglas, assayer for the Copper Queen Mining company and later president of the Phelps Dodge Corporation, Douglas (elev. 3984') came into existence in 1901 when Phelps Dodge moved their smelters to this site from Bisbee. Several buildings are worth seeing, beginning with the Gadsden Hotel, a 1907 landmark that is a registered National Historic Monument. This 160-room hotel, with its opulent main lobby, still operates as a hotel and even gives reduced rates (as do some Douglas motels) for members of the GABA ride. Another excellent building is the old El Paso and Southwestern railroad depot, which stands just west of the main business district. Its sister station, at the western end of the line, now serves as a familiar downtown Tucson restaurant — Carlos Murphy's.

You also should ride into the residential area east of downtown Douglas. There you will find many homes constructed for upper management employees of Phelps Dodge and other prosperous citizens.

Day Two — Douglas to Sierra Vista (50 miles)

Douglas to The Hub — The first 22.5 miles of your return ride are the same as the end of your first day's route. Ride from Douglas on the gradual uphill U.S. 80 past Double Adobe Road, up into the foothills of the Mule Mountains, and to The Hub, Bisbee's traffic circle. It was on this return trip from Douglas to Bisbee in 1990 that I last saw Gene Chapman, one of the best friends Tucson cyclists have ever had. He waved cheerily to me as I began to pump up the foothills, and I will remember that wave whenever I think of him, because he died a few weeks later.

At The Hub, take the first right and head up the hill to downtown Bisbee, 1.7 miles away. On your left is the seemingly bottomless Lavender Pit, named not for its purplish hues but rather for a mining company official.

Bisbee to the top of Mule Pass — You can take two routes through Bisbee: the highway or Tombstone Canyon. I strongly recommend leaving the highway for two reasons: Tombstone Canyon has far more charm, and it avoids the Mule Pass Tunnel, which is one of the most unpleasant places to ride in Southern Arizona.

So, take the first Bisbee exit and follow the main street to the town's delightful business district. For more information on Bisbee, consult Ride One of this chapter beginning with "Bisbee." In fact, if you have time and have not been to Bisbee before, you might consider taking a sightseeing route such as the one in the same ride that begins with "Following La Vuelta's Criterium."

Challenging La Vuelta's Hillclimb — Here's another reason to try Tombstone Canyon instead of the highway: you can get first-hand experience on a challenging race course, one taken by Greg Le Mond, Inga Thompson, Jeff Pierce, Janelle Parks, Thurlow Rogers, and other renowned cyclists by taking the time-trial hillclimb. It begins in front of the museum (once the Phelps Dodge headquarters) and ends 2.1 miles later, almost at the summit of Mule Pass. Just for fun, set your cyclometer's stopwatch function and see how long it takes you to climb those 2.1 miles.

On the way through the canyon, notice the variety of architectural styles of the commercial buildings, the homes clinging to hillsides, the garages built over drainage ditches. The route is a monument to ingenuity. You'll cross under the main highway and leave commercial Bisbee behind, eventually taking a switchback up along

Riding La Vuelta's Tombstone Canyon Hillclimb

the hillside. Be sure to glance to your right on occasion, as you'll have some beautiful views of Bisbee before you reach the summit.

Near the crest you'll see a finish line painted across the road. Check your time. As of the 1991 La Vuelta, the best time up this 2.1-mile, 700-foot-altitude-gain monster is 9 minutes and 29 seconds, by Mike Engleman in 1987. The women's record as of 1991 is 10:33, set in 1987 by Leslee Schenk. Sort of makes you feel rather mortal, doesn't it? On the other hand, Mr. or Ms. Average American might have to catch his or her breath just driving the son of a gun, so take a measure of pride in your accomplishment.

Mule Pass to State Route 90 — Now it is Free Time: 6.5 miles of downhill blur. From the top of Mule Pass you have a bumpy .6 miles to U.S. 80. Take a right at the stop sign and enjoy 5.9 miles of joyous descent. But please stay in control, making certain that glee does not overcome judgment. Turn left at the bottom of the hill at state route 90 (the main highway goes to Tombstone).

To Sierra Vista — You have now come 32.8 miles from Douglas. For the last 16.9 miles of your journey, refer to Ride Two of this chapter, beginning with "Back to the San Pedro and Sierra Vista," as that ride covers the same route.

The essential mileage from Douglas is:

Douglas to downtown Bisbee	24.1 miles
Bisbee to state route 90	8.7 miles
State route 90 to Sierra Vista	16.9 miles
Total	49.7 miles

When you arrive at your car, you will have ridden almost 50 miles today (and even more if you toured Bisbee) and a minimum of 107 miles on your overnight loop.

81

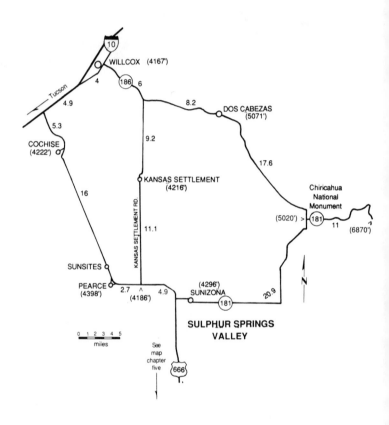

WILLCOX   (4167')

186

Tucson

4.9

5.3

COCHISE
(4222')

4

6

8.2

DOS CABEZAS
(5071')

9.2

17.6

16

KANSAS SETTLEMENT
(4216')

KANSAS SETTLEMENT RD.

11.1

Chiricahua
National
Monument

(5020') > 181   11
(6870')

SUNSITES

PEARCE
(4398')

2.7 ^
(4186')

4.9   (4296')
SUNIZONA

181

20.9

N

SULPHUR SPRINGS
VALLEY

0 1 2 3 4 5
miles

See
map
chapter
five

666

CHAPTER SIX
Sulphur Springs Valley

Willcox is a ranching and farming center only one-and-a-half hours from Tucson, and the excellent cycling should attract any road rider. Once again, here's a chapter with considerable diversity: a ride almost entirely on flat terrain, another with a stunning climb, one with wonderful variety, and one that is almost a century. And along the route you'll see farms and orchards, cattle country, ghost towns, pioneer cemeteries, the ruins of a stage station, the most enchanting hotel in Arizona, and a national monument with some of the most dramatic scenery in the state.

Willcox is the point of origin for all the rides. Named in 1880 for General Orlando B. Willcox, Commander of the Military Department stationed at Fort Whipple near Prescott, Willcox was an important center for the shipment of cattle and agricultural products. Now it might be best known as the home town of cowboy singer-actor Rex Allen, whose name graces a main street.

At almost 4200' elevation, Willcox is somewhat cooler than Tucson, and often you can have an enjoyable ride in the Sulphur Springs Valley when Tucson is getting a mite warm. Incidentally, don't just take your bike off your car and roar out of Willcox; be sure to tour the old section near the railroad tracks as there are several outstanding commercial buildings along with the 1880 Willcox railroad station, one of the best depots along the Southern Pacific line.

Every ride in this chapter is a day ride, but if you stay overnight, I strongly recommend the wonderful, historic Cochise Hotel (rooms and meals strictly by reservation only). For more about that hotel, see Ride Three, starting at "Cochise." If you do stay there, I suggest driving to Willcox for Ride One and riding from Cochise for Ride Three.

I drove to Willcox on a January Saturday morning, did Ride One, spent the night, and Mort Solot joined me on Sunday morning for Ride Three. I mention this because it was a weekend of great cycling and convinced me that two days of medium-to-long rides in the Sulphur Springs Valley are preferable to one totally exhausting day.

Moreover, if you don't spend the night, you won't have the unique experience of the Cochise Hotel.

Ride One — The Willcox Southeast Loop (86 miles)

The Willcox Southeast Loop is the ride of variety mentioned in the introduction to this chapter. You'll get flat country, rolling hills, a ghost town, and perhaps a long climb into a national monument.

Willcox to Dos Cabezas — Leave your car near Railroad Park, which is one block south of the traffic light in the center of old Willcox. Cross the tracks and leave town on state route 186. The road is wide and has an adequate shoulder. To your left you'll have a good view of why Dos Cabezas ("Two Heads") Peak got its name. To your right will be the Willcox Playa (dry lake), which sometimes floods, although it is very shallow even when full. During World War II, pilots of an amphibious aircraft attempted a landing there, and the plane was stuck for three months.

At 6 miles you'll pass Kansas Settlement Road, which is a turn you would take for Ride Three. This time, however, just follow the signs to Dos Cabezas and the Chiricahua National Monument. The shoulder narrows, and soon you'll be making a gradual, then a not-so-gradual climb into the foothills of the Dos Cabezas Mountains.

At about 12.5 miles into your ride, you can look up to the north and see that from here Dos Cabezas has become Una Cabeza.

Adobe ruins at Dos Cabezas

Dos Cabezas — Just before you enter the town of Dos Cabezas, at 14.2 miles from Willcox, you'll see, on your right, the town cemetery, which has some interesting markers.

Dos Cabezas (elev. 5071') was originally called Ewell Springs and in 1851 served as a base camp for a group surveying the boundary between the United States and Mexico. In 1857 the San Antonio and San Diego Stage Lines built a station at the site. The ruins are south of the highway on the east end of town on a dirt road.

The town's prosperity came from gold and silver deposits that were found in the Dos Cabezas range in the late 1870s. Several good adobe ruins stand along the highway as you pass through town. A few of those ruins have held up amazingly well considering that they have lost their roofs. Usually a collapsed roof means disaster for an adobe building, as rain will literally begin to melt the walls.

Dos Cabezas to Chiricahua National Monument — From Dos Cabezas the road narrows and becomes less smooth, but the scenery and terrain become much more interesting. At 22.9 miles into your ride you'll pass the turnoff to Ft. Bowie National Historic Site. By this point in the ride you'll have some attractive vistas of the Chiricahua Mountains ahead of you.

Turn off at the Riggs Cemetery, which is 29.3 miles from Willcox. It's a beautiful, peaceful, shady spot. The Riggs family pioneered this territory and own some 300 square miles of the valley. Ed Riggs (1885-1950) discovered many of the scenic wonders of the vicinity, and he and his wife Lillian were instrumental in having the area set aside as Chiricahua National Monument.

To Chiricahua National Monument — Just 2.5 miles beyond the Riggs Cemetery, state route 186 ends as it meets state route 181, which goes south to Sunizona and east into the national monument. Here it is decision time: if you are a very strong rider prepared for a long day of cycling, you might enjoy taking the left turn and riding into the monument. It's 22-miles out and back from here, with an altitude gain of almost 2000 feet. For further details and directions, consult Ride Two. For most riders, however, Ride One is plenty challenging at 86 miles.

On to Sunizona — State route 181 heading south gives you more varied views of the Chiricahuas and the Sulphur Springs Valley. You'll eventually take a right turn and head due west on a steady, quick downhill, going past occasional isolated homes and the Ash Creek School before you finally arrive at the junction of 181 and U.S. 666 near the settlement of Sunizona (elev. 4296').

Turn right (north) on U.S. 666. In February of 1991, three establishments that I had patronized on earlier rides — including a restaurant, an ice cream stand, and a market — were out of business. If they're closed, you have about 16 miles to sustenance.

From Sunizona the road traverses slightly hilly terrain. In just under 5 miles, at 59.7 miles into your ride, Kansas Settlement Road meets 666 (elev. 4186'). Turn right (unless you are taking Ride Four, the Willcox Grand Loop). This arrow-straight, flat road cuts nine miles off the Grand Loop and gives you another different aspect of the Sulphur Springs Valley, for Kansas Settlement Road could have been transported from the Midwest.

Kansas Settlement — This small community, 11.1 miles north of U.S. 666, was settled in 1910 by homesteaders from (surprise!) Kansas. At 4216', it is only slightly higher than Willcox; you have an easy, flat ride for the last leg of the loop. Brown's Country Store might look very welcome at this point.

Back to Willcox — Ride north from Kansas Settlement for 9.2 miles. The biggest event in that stretch will probably be a curve in the road as you leave town. At 80 miles on the loop you will return to state route 186. Turn left and ride the final 6 miles into Willcox. On the way back to town, look up at the Dos Cabezas Mountains and over at the Willcox Playa — they should look quite different in afternoon light from what you saw in the morning.

Ride Two — Chiricahua National Monument (22 miles or more)

Writing about cycling in Southern Arizona is easy because the area is perfect for the sport. Not too many states in the country can boast of Arizona's spectacular scenery, and (with all due respect to Prescott, Flagstaff, and Show Low) no area in Arizona can match our portion of the state for delightful year-round cycling.

Here is the most beautiful paved-road cycling in this book. For glorious scenery on a short ride, nothing else compares.

Before I visited the Chiricahuas years ago, I read a book by Weldon Heald, in which he called his beloved mountains "Sky Island," also the title of his book. I tried to imagine what he felt for this range, but even his vivid description did not prepare me for the experience that is the Chiricahuas, and nothing I can write here comes as close as Heald did. I have hiked the trails, explored the ghost towns, seen the sun frame the small town of Portal as I waited for the javelina, deer, coatamundi, and hummingbirds to appear. These are all part of the Chiricahuas, and yet they are mere fragments of the total experience. And I am a novice compared to those who know Sky Island.

What occurred here that makes the place so special? Geologically, one can only speculate. The principal theory holds that volcanic eruptions resulted in a 2,000-foot layer of rhyolite that became the Chiricahua Mountains. Then the natural artisans — water and wind — went inexorably to work. The result (incomplete, of course, in the scheme of things) is a remarkable array of balancing rocks, pedestals, and pinnacles that man tries to make sense of by giving identifiable shapes to. The overall effect is a sort of unending, amorphous Easter Island of magnificent, inconclusive form.

The Chiricahua Apaches depended upon this area long before the white man tried to describe it. This was the territory of one of the West's great heroes, Cochise, and one of its original rebels, Geronimo. The Chiricahua and the Dragoon mountains were their homeland, and, later, their refuge from the endless procession of the white settlers intruding upon their domain. For a better appreciation of their history and the white man's efforts to control them (and of one white man's efforts to befriend them), read Elliott Arnold's *Blood Brother*.

Options — Here are four variations of this beautiful ride:

1. You can ride from Willcox (86 miles) or Dos Cabezas (58 miles) and return the same direction you came.

2. You can do it as its own ride, leaving your car at the junction of state routes 181 and 186 for a distance of 22 miles.

3. You can add this ride to Ride 1, the Willcox Southeast Loop, for a total distance of 108 miles.

4. If you are an extremely strong rider, you could even add it to Ride 3, the Willcox Grand Loop, for a distance of 117 miles.

What do I really recommend? Start from Dos Cabezas. If you have read the description of Ride One, you know that the Willcox Southeast Loop becomes much more interesting from Dos Cabezas on, and the total distance (58 miles) is more reasonable than the much longer rides, considering the difficulty of riding up to the top of Chiricahua National Monument.

If you take that advice, drive to Dos Cabezas and follow the directions of Ride One from "Dos Cabezas" through "Turnoff to Chiricahua National Monument." Then continue below.

Into the Monument — From the junction of state routes 181 and 186 (elev. 5020') you'll begin a gentle, three-mile climb up to the park's entrance (elev. 5150'). The entrance fee for bikes at this writing is $1.00. You'll get a brochure that you'll want to put into your jersey pocket for easy reference along the way. Immediately inside the entrance is the Erickson Cemetery.

The Ericksons, like the Riggs (mentioned in Ride One), were pioneers. Neil Erickson came to the United States to join the army and fight Indians because his father had been killed by Indians while working on a railroad crew in Minnesota. Erickson served in the army from 1881 to 1886, during the Arizona campaign against Geronimo. After he left the army, Erickson and his wife Emma homesteaded a farm and cattle ranch in Bonita Canyon in the Chiricahua Mountains. Eventually Erickson lost his animosity towards the Indians as he came to understand that the Apaches who lived in the Chiricahuas were simply fighting for their survival.

Neil Erickson became the first forest ranger in the Chiricahuas, serving for 25 years. The Ericksons' daughter Lillian married Ed Riggs, and the two of them transformed the homestead into a prosperous guest ranch called Faraway Ranch, because it was located so "god-awful far away from everything." It was principally because of Ed and Lillian Riggs that the area became a national monument.

On to the Visitor Center — After the Erickson Cemetery, the next attraction, off a clearly marked turnoff to the left, is the retored two-story main residence of Faraway Ranch. On the main road, the Visitor Center, 2.3 miles from the park's entrance, stands at 5400' and has displays, a slide show, books, maps, restrooms, and water.

The pinnacles of Bonita Canyon in Chiricahua National Monument

To Massai Point — From the Visitor Center, the scenery turns from beautiful to spectacular. The road climbs along Bonita Canyon, and the wind- and rain-carved pinnacles lining the way are breathtaking. So is the uphill; take your time and enjoy the views. The road is narrow, so be on the lookout for oversized vehicles, even though people tend to drive through here at a very moderate pace. Several turnouts along the route will give you places to rest and create your own names for the unique rock formations.

You will leave Bonita Canyon for the last part of the ascent, a twisting mountain road. You'll have some majestic views of the eastern side of the Chiricahuas and across into New Mexico. In 6.7 miles from the Visitor Center you'll come to Massai Point (elev. 6870').

Massai Point was named for Big Foot Massai, an Apache warrior who in 1890 escaped from a prison-bound trainload of Indians and was observed stealing a horse, which was later found at what is now Massai Point. The warrior was never seen again. The point named after him has dramatic views in all directions. A circular exhibit building at the end of a short trail gives you information about the peaks you can see from this vantage point, including a striking view of Cochise Head, a formation that really does look like a reclining human.

The ride back down is, of course, virtually effortless. Be extremely cautious on the blind curves and be on the lookout once again for motorhomes and vehicles with wide mirrors.

Ride Three — The Willcox Southwest Loop (61 miles)

You don't like hills? This ride, along with the Coolidge Century of Chapter Two, is for you. But the Willcox Southwest Loop has other attractions as well: adequate food stops despite the sparse population; good views of the Dos Cabezas, Chiricahua, and Dragoon mountains; and two ghost towns, each with remarkable buildings. The directions start from Willcox; if you are leaving from Cochise, begin with the section at the end of this ride, "Cochise to Willcox."

Willcox to Kansas Settlement to U.S. 666 — Beginning at Railroad Park in downtown Willcox, follow state route 186 out of town for 6 miles. Turn right on Kansas Settlement Road and ride for 9.2 miles to the small community of Kansas Settlement, homesteaded in 1910 by Jayhawkers. Continue south for 11.1 miles to U.S. 666 and turn right. You may find more traffic along U.S. 666 than you did on Kansas Settlement Road, but the lanes are adequate and visibility is excellent.

Pearce — In 2.7 miles, you'll have a decision to make: how to get to Pearce. The shorter way takes the dirt road that continues west as the highway makes a turn to the northwest. It's a solid-packed, rideable road that I have taken with many people, and it only lasts three-quarters of a mile. Riding it saves 1.8 miles, and it passes close to the remnants of the last great gold strike in Arizona's history: James Pearce's Commonwealth Mine. If you are hesitant to take the dirt road, you can ride up to the paved turnoff and return to Pearce. You might have a temptation to forget the backtrack and omit the town, but take it from the many out-of-state cyclists I have taken on a journey through this valley: don't miss Pearce.

In 1894 James Pearce was resting on top of Six Mile Hill not far from his and his brother's ranch. There he discovered a rich outcropping of gold ore; in the next eight years his Commonwealth claim produced $30 million in gold.

At one time Pearce (elev. 4398') was a thriving community with rows of falsefront stores, municipal buildings, and homes. Now only a whisper of that boom town remains. A school, the old post office, some adobe ruins and foundations, a church, a jail, and a cemetery west of town — these would be enough to make a visit to Pearce interesting. But there also is a treasure: a large 1894 adobe building known as The Old Store.

The Old Store — Once a general merchandise, later a museum, The Old Store in Pearce is one of the best structures remaining in the West. You will be cycling right by it, but aficionados of Western Americana drive hundreds of miles out of their way to see it. The store used to contain thousands of items of antiquity, but much of the collection has been sold. The Old Store, nevertheless, will remain a

The Old Store at Pearce

remarkable remnant of the Old West for as long as it stands. The dirt road heading south leads to a ghost town mountain bike excursion (Chapter Eight, Ride One).

North from Pearce — Take the paved road north from The Old Store. The bunker-like building on your left was the town jail. Turn left on U.S. 666; in just over a mile (and 32 miles on your loop from Willcox) you'll be in Arizona Sunsites, a small community with cafes and a convenience store. In 5.4 miles you'll pass another store.

The dominant manmade feature along this route will be the coal-fired Apache Power Station with its set of flashing strobe lights. It's easy to get nearly hypnotized by the lights as you head toward them for miles. You'll finally pass the plant at 42 miles into your loop and 12.2 miles north of Pearce. North of the plant 2.3 miles is the Cochise Cemetery on your left, and 1.5 miles beyond the cemetery is the turnoff for the .7-mile paved route into Cochise. Even if you're not staying here for the night, you simply must take a look.

Cochise — The town of Cochise (elev. 4222') was a rail-stop at the junction of the Southern Pacific and the long-defunct Arizona Eastern railroads. The trains carried ore and supplies to the nearby mining towns of Johnson and Pearce, and Cochise itself served the needs of ranches in the area. As you enter the quiet main street, you'll see homes, a closed-up church, a school, the post office, and, where the street ends at a "T," two exceptional buildings. On the right is the Cochise Country Store, occupied but closed for business at this writing, and, on your left, the marvelous Cochise Hotel.

The Cochise Hotel and its inviting front porch

The Cochise Hotel — Built in 1882, the Cochise Hotel, like The Old Store in Pearce, is absolutely unique. It originally served railroad travelers and employees, and now it can serve you. The hotel has only five rooms, three with double-beds and two "suites," which have an additional small room with a single bed. Each room contains authentic 1880s furnishings, so you really will feel as if you've slipped back in time. It is not really the purpose of this book to recommend one place of business over another, but this hotel offers such a wonderful experience that I can't help but tell you to phone ahead (384-3156) and make reservations. When you do, you will be asked an important question — "Chicken or steak?" — which refers to dinner that night (I have enjoyed both but am partial to the chicken). Also included is breakfast the next morning.

I have taken numerous groups to the Cochise Hotel, including ghost town classes and bicycling tours. Because these are people out for adventure and the unusual, they have loved the hotel. All right, so the bathrooms aren't the Hilton, but the authenticity of the place more than makes up for any lack of luxury. And to stroll through town after dinner and then to sit on the porch of the hotel and watch trains go by as the sun sets is one of the real pleasures on the planet.

[note: Here is one piece of bicycling etiquette at the hotel. You may not bring your bike into your room, so don't ask; it will be stored in a shed where bikes have safely rested for all our visits.]

Cochise to Willcox — Riding from Cochise to Willcox, a distance of 15 miles, requires traveling on the interstate, and, although it's not pleasant, it's legal and bearable. Leave Cochise, turn left (north) on U.S. 666, and ride for 5.3 miles to I-10. Along the way you'll climb the overpass for the Southern Pacific; the view of the tracks traversing the Willcox Playa is positively surreal. The shoulder of I-10 has cuts in the road to alert dozing motorists, but you can ride to the right of them easily.

Turn off the interstate 4.9 miles after entering, at Exit 336, the first of three Willcox exits. Proceed on this road for 4 miles to downtown Willcox. Turn right at the stoplight and go to the park by the railroad tracks, where you either left your car this morning, if you started from Willcox, or, if you spent the night in Cochise, where you will now turn back to the beginning of this ride for directions on the Willcox Southwest Loop.

Ride Four — The Willcox Grand Loop (95 miles)

If you're determined to see the best of the Sulphur Springs Valley in only one day, this loop combines the best of Rides One and Three, eliminating the Kansas Settlement Road section of both rides. If you are what Mort calls a "Superjock," you may even add Ride Two, into the Chiricahua National Monument, to make a 117-mile ride. My concern is that the person who tries to accomplish all this in a day will miss the beauty of the area in the dash for the distance.

Directions: Follow Ride One through mile 59.7, but do not turn right on Kansas Settlement Road. Instead, turn to Ride Three and begin with "Kansas Settlement Road and U.S. 666." Follow Ride Three back to Willcox.

CHAPTER SEVEN
Mountain Bike Rides Near Tucson

When I bought my first mountain bike in the Spring of 1982, I had to go to Phoenix — there wasn't one yet available in Tucson. I first climbed the Oracle to Mount Lemmon road on Memorial Day of that year, and my fellow rider and I were greeted with looks of disbelief by inhabitants of four-wheel-drive vehicles on the way. Now, of course, the mountain bike is a common sight.

Mountain bikers, I believe, are looking for different information than road cyclists. The back roads rider isn't going to be stopping at restaurants and is not as likely to be concerned about road conditions or overnight spots. In fact, my experience has been that mountain bikers want only "bare bones" information to complete the ride— the rest they want to discover on their own.

As a result, this chapter and Chapter Eight will be much less detailed than the previous six road bike chapters. For more specific information about other rides, consult a book specializing in mountain bike rides. I recommend *Southern Arizona Fat Tire Guide,* by R. Conway, T. Fischer, and D. Vick.

Instead of providing maps for each ride, I'll list the topographic maps or area maps that will help you on your route. But you don't need to buy them: you can photocopy topographic maps in the basement of the University of Arizona Library (the maps are in the public domain and copying them is quite legal).

Ride One — Tucson Mountain Park

Level of Difficulty — varies, from easy to very technical
Topographic Map — 1968 (photorevised 1975) Cat Mountain 7.5'
Area Map — Tucson Mountain Regional Park

One of the crucial conflicts between mountain bikers and hikers is trail accessibility. I am one who believes that in most locations the cyclist, equestrian, and hiker do not belong on the same trail. I have quite unintentionally scared the wits out of both horse and rider, and I have no desire to repeat the experience. Nevertheless, I also believe that under certain circumstances all three trail users can coexist. In Tucson Mountain Regional Park, only a few minutes' ride from downtown Tucson, such a coexistence is a reality.

The best way to explore Tucson Mountain Park is to have with you the area map that is available from Pima County Parks and Recreation at the Administrative Headquarters, 1204 W. Silverlake. At this writing the price for this oversize map is $3.00. A favorite place to begin is the David Yetman Trail Head at the southern end of Camino De Oeste, south of Gates Pass Road (turn south just west of Scordato's restaurant). The Yetman Trail takes you for 6.1 miles over easy-to-challenging terrain to a junction of trails. One popular route is to continue south by joining the Starr Pass Trail, which skirts through a canyon at the base of Cat Mountain.

Another possibilty is to stay on the Yetman Trail by going west at the intersection and come out at the western base of Gates Pass. I've always had to walk some of this route, as parts are quite sandy, but I'm sure riders with more technical prowess than I can make it.

An easy and enjoyable trail ride is the Golden Gate Trail, which follows the western slope of Golden Gate Mountain. In addition, west of Old Tucson is a power line trail that is a real treat. It dead ends, but it's fun while it lasts.

Actually, the best thing to do in Tucson Mountain Regional Park is to strike out on your own (but always staying on trails), as you will find many favorite variations that suit your desire for adventure.

Ride Two — Redington Road and Chiva Falls

Level of Difficulty — *easy (Redington Road) to very challenging (the route to the falls)*
Topographic Maps — *1981 Agua Caliente Hill 7.5'; 1981 Piety Hill 7.5'*

Tucson to the Rincons — Drive to the east end of Tanque Verde Road until the road turns to dirt (elev. 2829'). I've parked here and ridden the steep, twisting ascent into the Rincon Mountains. But on weekends you may opt to drive up a few miles until you are well past the traffic jam that often forms on the way to popular Seven Falls. If you do drive up, a logical place to park your vehicle is near the cattle pens that you'll see about 4.7 miles from where you left the pavement. Whether you ride or drive, that parking area (elev. 3930') is the place from which to base your mileage to Chiva Falls.

On to Chiva Falls — From the cattle pens, ride Redington Road for 3.6 miles; there turn right and cross a cattleguard on a much more rugged road than the one you've been on. After 3.0 miles of often rather technical riding, you will come to a "Y" in the trail. Stay on the left, but remember the place, as you will take the other road going out. In .5 miles after the junction, you'll see some

Chiva Falls — dry on this visit

sparse adobe ruins on your right that one source says was a stage stop (elev. 3760').

In 1.4 miles after the ruin (and after some very rugged riding) you'll come to the end of the ridable trail. Chiva (Spanish for "goat")

Falls and its inviting pool (elev. 4000') are just ahead.

When you return, remember to take the left fork at the "Y". From there it's 2.5 miles of tough riding back to your vehicle.

Ride Three — Charouleau Gap

Level of Difficulty — *Challenging, occasionally rather technical*

Topographic Maps — *1988 Oracle 7.5'; 1988 Oracle Junction 7.5'*

This is one of the favorite time-trial races of Tucson's growing number of mountain bike competitors. I found climbing to the Charouleau (local pronunciation, "shar-loo") Gap plenty of work even taking as long as I needed; to race against time on such a course is something I don't even want to think about. I have a lot of respect for those guys.

Getting to the Start — Drive north from Tucson on Oracle Road, heading toward the town of Catalina. Turn right (east) on Golder Ranch Road. Turn left in 1.2 miles at Lago del Oro Parkway (just before the bridge on Golder Ranch Road). Drive north for 2.3 miles to Edwin. You could drive farther, but I suggest parking here so you can have a bit of warm-up riding before you begin your ascent. From here to Charouleau Gap is six miles.

Climbing to the Gap — Ride east on Edwin, following it around a bend where to go straight would be to enter private property. You'll cross Cañada del Oro Wash (elev. 3150') and follow the

This cattleguard and fence post tell you you've reached The Gap

main dirt road as it immediately begins to climb up the other side of the wash. For most of the route the road is not technically difficult — but it's certainly uphill with some very steep grades. At several places the neophyte needs two or three runs at certain sections, while experienced riders seem to make all the right moves.

The scenery is terrific: you can see the town of Catalina to the west-northwest, and more to the north you'll eventually have a fine view of Biosphere 2, the self-contained miniature earth environment.

After some killer climbs and a final steep ascent around some switchbacks, you'll come to a fence and cattleguard that mark the actual Gap (elev. 5080'). The road continues on from there, eventually going into private property. The time trial ends at the Gap, and I was perfectly happy to have water and a snack while I savored the thought of the downhill return. Incidentally, don't forget to let some air out of your tires and lower your seat post for the trip back. On some of the steepest grades, be certain to keep in control as you careen back toward the wash.

A controlled descent from Charouleau Gap

Ride Four — Oracle to Mt. Lemmon

Level of Difficulty *— Difficult, mostly because of the distance and the climb. There isn't much technical riding except for the treacherous downhills back to Oracle.*

Topographic Maps *— 1988 Oracle 7.5'; 1948 (photo revised 1972) Campo Bonito 7.5'; 1981 Mt. Bigelow 7.5'; 1981 Mt. Lemmon 7.5'*

Here are a couple of ways to do this challenging ride: You can leave your car in Oracle and do an up-and-back to Mt. Lemmon; or, if you have someone who can drop you off in Oracle, you can ride to the top and come down the paved Mt. Lemmon highway back into Tucson. Either way it's going to be about 60 miles. Going back to Oracle is the much more difficult route, because, as any mountain biker knows, blowing downhill on a twisting, rocky dirt road is hard, jarring work. But it is also great fun. Going back via the paved road is virtually effortless, but you might have to deal with a serious hazard: the impatient and/or impaired driver.

Oracle to Peppersauce — Drive to Oracle (elev. 4513'), about 28 miles from the intersection of Ina and Oracle in northwest Tucson. Ride the paved Mt. Lemmon Road heading east-southeast out of town. It will turn to dirt in a couple of miles. Take the right fork beyond the end of the pavement. Shortly after, you'll pass the site of the old town of American Flag, now headquarters for an working ranch. After about 5 miles you'll come to Peppersauce Campground (elev. 4651'). A popular time-trial loop starts from here, but our ride will follow the main road.

You've gone over 5 miles and you've gained only 138 feet. From Peppersauce you'll begin a climb to over 4800' only to descend, over the next 10 miles, to under 4300'. So here you are, 15 miles into your ride, and you've actually lost altitude from Oracle. But you will also see that the big challenge is now about to commence.

The Struggle to the Top — You will climb from 4296' to over 7800' in the next 12 or so miles. You'll pass mine workings, enter a cool pine forest, and occasionally enjoy some spectacular vistas. The road deteriorates as it climbs, and there may be spots too steep, rocky, or soft to negotiate. But it is an exhilarating feeling of accomplishment to pass the old sawmill and reach the pavement.

The Descent — I've done this both ways. If you're returning down the back way to Oracle, take special care for the first steep and rough miles. If you head to Tucson, be on the lookout for motorists and road construction. With either route, control your speed.

Ride Five — Saguaro National Monument's Cactus Forest Trail

Level of Difficulty — *moderate, with some technical spots*
Topographic Map — *1981 Tanque Verde Peak 7.5' (but*
the route is not marked, so it is of no help here)
Additional Map — *Park Service Brochure*

In June of 1991, Park Superintendent William F. Paleck of Saguaro National Monument gave the mountain bikers of Tucson a terrific present — with a couple of well-advised strings attached. Paleck opened a portion of the Cactus Forest Trail, in the East District of the Monument, to cyclists on a trial basis. This is the first sharing of a multi-use trail in the entire park system, and it's a privilege to ride it. The aformentioned strings were that continued sharing of the trail would depend upon cyclists' behavior on the trail and an assessment of any damage their bikes might cause.

The section open to cyclists cuts across the paved monument loop (see Chapter One, Ride One) for the longest section of the Cactus Forest Trail. Its 3.5-mile distance is just enough for you to want much more, so here's hoping that riders are courteous on the trail and that perhaps more sections will eventually be open. The trail continues on either end of the section open to you at this writing, but don't be tempted to take it, as on those sections you are currently prohibited. Incidentally, the trail is occasionally patrolled by a ranger on a mountain bike graciously donated by Full Cycle's Chuck Kohler.

I recommend starting at the southern end of the trail for three reasons: one, it's a gentler beginning than the northern end, so riders can become accustomed to trail riding more readily; two, you ride much less pavement to get to the trailhead; and three, when you arrive at the northern end, you have two pleasant options— turning right and completing the paved loop, or doing what I do: I turn around and hit the trail again.

To get to the southern end, ride past the entrance kiosk and turn right. As you head down a hill .9 miles from the kiosk, you'll see a sign clearly marking the Cactus Forest Trail. Turn left and begin your single-track adventure.

The route is narrow, and parts of it are so easy that you may get lulled into complacency, but stay alert because hikers and/or equestrians may appear, and, because it is a trail and not a road, the route offers many surprise turns, dips, sandy washes, and small logs placed across the trail to slow erosion. Keep your speed to under 10 mph to allow for such unexpected events. But more than that, keep your speed down to control erosion (wide turns tear up the desert, fast turns cause unnecessary ruts) and to enjoy the reason you're there in the first place: to savor the wonderful desert scenery.

Negotiating Slick Rock near Charouleau Gap

CHAPTER EIGHT

Mountain Bike Rides of Southern Arizona

These are some favorite rides I've taken with friends over the past several years in Southern Arizona. As in Chapter Seven, the routes will be given in less detail than road bike chapters. Here are some new destinations; you plan the specifics.

Ride One — Pearce, Courtland, and Gleeson

Level of Difficulty — easy
Topographic Maps — 1985 Pearce 7,5'; 1985 Turquoise Mtn. 7.5'; 1958 Outlaw Mtn. 7.5'

This pleasant ride of under 30 miles connects three of the better ghost towns in Southern Arizona.

Pearce (elev. 4400') is 94 miles southeast of Tucson just off U.S. 666. The last of the Arizona gold rush camps, Pearce was founded in 1894. The best building in town is The Old Store, a large falsefront adobe building. Leave your car in town and ride the back streets, making certain to view the cemetery (west of town on the Middlemarch Road), the school, the old post office, and the church. The ruins on the side of the hill to the southeast are what's left of the workings of the Commonwealth, the mine that gave Pearce its life.

Courtland (elev. 4790') is nine miles south of Pearce. A town that lasted from 1909 until 1942, Courtland has only two standing buildings, both near the road. The first is the jail, which you'll see on your left as the road turns toward the west. Continue down the road .5 miles, where you'll see the walls of a store on your right.

Gleeson (elev. 4923') is the most interesting site for the mountain biker. Continue south from Courtland for just over three miles and turn right. In one mile, as you enter Gleeson, you'll see the adobe walls of the hospital on your right and the wonderful arch of the school on your left. West of the school stands the Gleeson jail, a twin of the one you saw in Courtland. The cemetery is west of town on the dirt road that continues 15 miles to U.S. 80 and Tombstone.

Hospital ruins at Gleeson

Named for Pearce prospector John Gleeson, the town prospered from 1909 until 1939, the year the post office closed. The last mine shut down in 1953. Several roads may interest you here, such as the one up to some of the major workings northeast of town. The road heading south from the jail was once the main route to Bisbee. And the dirt road heading north goes past the Musso house, now a crumbling adobe, which once was Gleeson's most elaborate home. It was rumored that during Prohibition the Mussos hid liquor in a vault under their backyard fishpond. It was probably more than rumor: the shallow concrete pond and hollow space underneath, now filled with debris, were quite apparent in the 1980s.

Ride Two — Harshaw, Mowry, Washington Camp, and Duquesne

Level of Difficulty *— easy, with some moderate climbs*
Topographic Maps *— 1958 Harshaw 7.5'; 1958*
   Duquesne 7.5'

The road heading south out of Patagonia (elev. 4035'), a charming small town about 65 miles from mid-town Tucson, is a mountain biking favorite for Southern Arizonans. And for good reason: the road goes through lovely country with some interesting ghost towns, and the temperature is several degrees cooler than Tucson.

Harshaw (elev. 4816'), named for cattleman and miner David Tecumseh Harshaw, was founded in 1877. The remnants of the town stand 9 miles south of Patagonia on a road that is paved for almost 8 miles. You might park your car where the road turns to dirt and ride from there. When you reach the Harshaw townsite, notice the small cemetery up on the hill to your right. Take the road branching to your left to see two cabins and a beautiful wood and brick home with a graceful tin porch roof. An occupied home with outbuildings also stands along this side road.

Mowry (elev. 5408') is 5 miles south of Harshaw on the main dirt road. At the Forest Service sign, turn left to explore the townsite, which contains several adobe walls and a large slag dump from an old smelter. Sylvester Mowry owned the lead and silver Patagonia Mine at this site, but when he was accused of being a Confederate sympathizer, his property was seized. He spent several months in the Yuma Territorial Prison. Although released for lack of evidence, he never did get his mine back.

Washington Camp (elev. 5375') stands 5 miles south of Mowry. The town shows little of its antiquity. Its sister town of **Duquesne** (elev. 5360') is the better ghost town, and the route to Duquesne, which leaves the main dirt road just south of Washington Camp and heads up a hill to the right, offers a bit more of a challenge than the roads you've been riding.

Company office or barracks at Duquesne

103

Duquesne and Washington Camp were company towns of the Duquesne Mining and Reduction Company. The post office switched from one town to the other from 1880 until 1920. Duquesne's several wooden buildings are clearly marked against trespassers, but you can get a good view from the road.

If you parked your car 8 miles south of Patagonia, you will have ridden about 12 miles so far. You could turn around in Duquesne or ride 3 more miles south to the tiny border community of Lochiel (elev. 4675'). Along that route stands a memorial to Fray Marcos de Niza, who in 1539 crossed into what became the United States.

Ride Three — Mount Hopkins

Level of Difficulty — not technical, but definitely uphill
Topographic Map — 1981 Mt. Hopkins 7.5'

This is a terrific 25-mile ride if you want a challenging climb on an excellent dirt road, if you like marvelous vistas, and if you want to do literally all of your work in the first half of your miles for the day. Drive south from Tucson on I-19, exiting at Canoa Road, 4 miles south of Green Valley's Continental Road exit. Cross under the interstate, turn right, and go 3.3 miles to Elephant Head Road and turn left. In 1.4 miles turn right and proceed to the Smithsonian Visitors' Center. *[note: 4.5 miles from Elephant Head Road is Bull Springs Road, the point of origin for the next ride in this chapter.]* Your ride begins just beyond the Visitors' Center, where the pavement ends.

On your drive up to the Smithsonian, you'll have a good, long look at the MMT, the multi-mirror telescope that is perched on the top of Mount Hopkins. If you are unaccustomed to long mountain climbs, the telescope might look hopelessly out of reach— but it isn't.

Leave your car in the parking lot and ride into Montosa Canyon. Your beginning altitude is 4260'. The road is excellent but the grade is relentless. For 12 miles you'll climb for the summit of Mt. Hopkins (8585)'. There may be a closed gate before the last attack to the top, but you can simply put your bike through. When I last rode the route, there was no sign prohibiting bikes, and, in fact, we were greeted warmly by MMT personnel and given a tour of the facilities. Mort and I first took this ride in July of 1983, riding 19 miles from the town of Amado, as there was no paved road or visitors' center. When Mort signed the visitors' book, he also wrote "by bicycle." An employee said we might be the first people to have ridden up.

The return trip is incredible. Just be certain to control your speed and watch carefully for oncoming vehicles at blind corners.

Ride Four — Bull Springs Road, Josephine Canyon, and the Salero Road

Level of Difficulty — easy (Salero Road) to technical
(Josephine Canyon)
Topographic Maps — 1981 Mt. Hopkins 7.5', 1981 San Cayetano Mtns. 7.5'; 1981 Patagonia 7.5'

As mentioned in the previous entry, The Bull Springs ride begins on the road to Mt. Hopkins. From Tucson, follow the directions given in Ride Three. Bull Springs Road heads south from the paved Mt. Hopkins road 4.5 miles from Elephant Head Road. Leave your vehicle at that point (elev. 3820'). *[**Terrific option:** If you know a person who is a candidate for sainthood, have him or her drop you off and wait in Patagonia, which is 27 mountain bike miles away.]*

I like this ride for several reasons: it covers an interesting variety of roads from wide and fast to tedious and technical; I've experienced virtually no traffic on any of four visits; and, finally, as a local rancher once told me, "There's history in those hills."

For the first part of Bull Springs Road you'll be on a wide, easily negotiable road, but by the time you pass the Glove Mine (elev. 4260') on your left at about 5 miles, the route will have begun to deteriorate. You'll soon begin the first of several good climbs. From now on you'll be skirting the foothills of the Santa Ritas; in this varied terrain you'll practically forget what a level road looks like.

Josephine Canyon — About 11 miles into your ride you'll come to an intersection (elev. 5180'). To the left is a drop into Josephine Canyon, where technical riding awaits. To the right is the road to Salero, a road that seems like a highway compared to what you've been on. I'd recommend going into Josephine Canyon for a look at some wonderful country. *[note: If you left your vehicle on Mt. Hopkins Road, this might be a good place to turn around.]*

Alto — Down the Salero Road 2.5 miles are the ruins of the post office built in 1907 at what is now the ghost town of Alto (elev. 4600'). Gold and lead discoveries created the town, but the mines were shut down by 1933, the year the post office closed.

Post office ruins at Alto

Salero — The Salero Ranch (elev. 4273') will be on your right when you have ridden 2.2 miles from Alto. South of the ranch 1.7 miles is a turnoff, marked clearly with "no trespassing" signs, that leads to the ghost town of Salero. You can view the town from a hill near the road if you park your bike and climb a short rise.

"Salero" is "saltcellar" in Spanish, and a legend says that the mine was named for a saltcellar, fashioned from the mine's silver, that decorated the dinner table for a bishop visiting the mission at Tumacacori. Two workers for the Salero Mining Company, John Wrightson and Gilbert Hopkins, were killed by Apaches in the 1860s; they are remembered today because their names grace the two highest peaks in the Santa Ritas — Mt. Wrightson and Mt. Hopkins.

From Salero — If you are returning to your car on Mt. Hopkins Road, you have 17 miles of adventure still to come. If you are going to Patagonia, all the tough riding is over. From Salero, ride 7.9 miles to the crossing of Sonoita Creek (elev. 3960') and join the pavement of state route 82 for a 3.5-mile ride to Patagonia.

Ride Five — The Ruby Road

Level of Difficulty — *not technical, but lots of good climbs and fast descents*
Topographic Maps — *1981 Peña Blanca Lake 7.5'; 1981 Ruby 7.5'; 1979 Arivaca 7.5'; 1979 Bartlett Mtn. 7.5'*

Ralph Phillips of Fairwheel Bikes had never taken a mountain bike ride. He put it off about as long as he could, in part, I think, because of the initial disdain that true road racers once had for the fat-tire bike. But finally he grabbed one off his showroom floor and headed out with Ned Mackey and me to take on the Ruby Road.

We drove south on I-19 to the Ruby Road turnoff (seven miles north of Nogales and about 64 miles from mid-town Tucson) and turned right to Peña Blanca Lake (9 miles west of I-19). There we left the truck and rode out (beginning elev. 3882'). This should be a good route for someone who is learning about the mountain bike because the road is wide and not too traveled, and the terrain is quite varied. Yet despite its relatively non-technical nature, the Ruby Road did eat us up and spit us out, as you will learn.

At about 9 miles from the lake you'll come to Hank and Yank Spring at the entrance to Sycamore Canyon (elev. 4030'). A Forest Service sign will tell you about the ranching efforts of Hank Hewitt and "Yank" Bartlett. Five miles beyond the spring is Ruby (elev. 4160'), one of Arizona's best ghost towns. When Ralph, Ned, and I were on our ride, I knew the caretaker and so was able to take them into the townsite. It is at this writing closed to the public except for tours arranged by Pima College. This is an excellent turnaround spot. From the gate you can see some of the town, which closed in 1941.

When we returned to Peña Blanca Lake, Ralph somewhat abashedly admitted that he had told his wife Martha that he was "going to take the day off and go mountain biking." He had not expected the workout we had received. We'd gone "only" 28 miles, yet Ned was nursing a cut hand from a fall; I had a sore rear end from hitting the saddle wrong on a skidding climb; Ralph was tired, dirty, and had an aching arm. The next day he found out the arm had a stress fracture. So much for "taking the day off."

But Ralph came back for more. A few months later he and Mary Ann Mead and I rode our bikes from Arivaca (elev. 3643') to Ruby to complete the route. This is a considerably flatter, much easier ride than from Peña Blanca Lake. Leave your car in Arivaca (64 miles southwest of mid-town Tucson) and head south on the main dirt road. At 9 miles into your ride you'll climb a small hill and to your right will be a stage stop built in the late 1870s at Oro Blanco (elev. 4002'). The building is on private ranch property. South of the ranch on a hill to the west stands the tiny Oro Blanco cemetery. Ruby is 4 miles south from there. Again, we turned around at Ruby for a 26-mile round trip.

An option not available to us would be to have someone drop you at Peña Blanca Lake and pick you up in Arivaca. This would be the best, most enjoyable route, as you would get the toughest part of the ride out of the way in the first 9 or so miles and save the easiest portion for the end of the tour.

Ride Six — Las Guijas

Level of Difficulty — *some sand, but overall fairly easy*
Topographic Map — *1979 Cerro Colorado 7.5'; 1979 Las Guijas 7.5'*

A friend told me about a ghost town somewhere near Arivaca and I realized it wasn't one I already knew about. When I determined from map work that it was Las Guijas, friends Tom Bartlett and Ralph Phillips and I mountain biked to the site.

Drive from Tucson to Arivaca Junction (41 miles from Tucson). Instead of going all the way to Arivaca, go 15 miles toward Arivaca and park your car at the turnoff to the Circle 46 Ranch. You will be going 7.7 miles on the main dirt road heading west.

Almost immediately after leaving your car you'll pass, on your left, the grave of John Poston, murdered by outlaws at the mine he was superintending for his brother Charles. The mining settlement that once stood here was Cerro Colorado (elev. 3558'), named for the red hill to the northeast. South of the grave, up over a small hill, are remnants of later mining efforts.

The road to Las Guijas crosses a wash of the same name. About .4 miles before the main townsite you'll see some foundations hidden in brush to your right. You will have arrived at Las Guijas (elev. 3480') when you see definite diggings on the hillside to your left and several foundations at a right turn in the road. "Guijas" means "con-glomerate" or "quartz pebbles" in Spanish and refers to the conglomerate in which gold was found here in the 1860s. It's also the name of the mountains immediately to the south.

Just beyond the site at the turn in the road you will see some more elaborate foundations and mill workings, but the best is ahead: Go down into Las Guijas Wash near the mill tailings (a fine sand). There, lying in a thick bed of the tailings, is an old panel truck from the 1930s or '40s. Look at the faint, stencilled letters on the sides and back door. The thing was a paddy wagon!

The Cerro Colorado and Las Guijas topographic maps show you other roads to pursue in the area, and we went over a few before returning to my truck. They were great to ride, but the treat of the day was Las Guijas and the old panel truck that reads "POLICE."

Ride Seven — Silver Bell to Sasco

Level of Difficulty — *from easy to as tough as you want it*
Topographic Maps — *1989 Silver Bell East 7.5'; 1989 Silver Bell West 7.5'; 1981 Samaniego Hills 7.5'*

Ride Seven of Chapter One takes you by road bike out to the ghost town of Silver Bell; Ride One of Chapter Two sends you past Red Rock. Here's a back roads ride connecting those two towns that features good dirt road riding (including part on an old railroad bed), lots of Arizona history, and a chance to explore an uninhabited old ghost town by mountain bike.

I've done versions of this ride many times and it comes down to this: I think the Silver Bell-Sasco Road is one of the most enjoyable desert back roads to ride close to Tucson. And Sasco has the best variety of desert riding I've ever experienced.

Here are three ways to consider doing this ride:

1. Ride from Silver Bell to Sasco and return (almost 40 miles, plus whatever miles you ride around Sasco).

2. Have someone drop you off in Silver Bell and pick you up in Sasco (19.8 miles) or Red Rock (26.5 miles).

3. Drive to Red Rock or Sasco (take a truck to Sasco) and ride the area (mileage varies depending how many back roads and trails you take. We have averaged 15-20 miles per visit.)

I have done #1 (once) and #3 (many times), but I've always wanted to do #2.

Version One — Silver Bell to Sasco

The sign at the end of the Avra Valley-Silver Bell road bike ride tells you that the road ahead is a dead end. Don't you believe it. The pavement may end, but the adventure for a mountain bike is just beginning. For this desert ride, drive north on I-10 to Exit 242 (Avra Valley Road) and head west for 23 miles to the Silver Bell Mine and the ghost town of the same name. For more information on Silver Bell, see Chapter One, Ride Seven, the first and fourth paragaphs.

The ghost town to your left (elev. 2628'), consisting of only a few standing buildings, is the second Silver Bell. Founded in 1948, it was closed down and dismantled in the mid-1980s. The original town, spelled Silverbell, was founded just after the turn of the century, although mining had been going on in the vicinity for more than 40 years. Incidentally, despite the name, the ore that made both Silverbells prosper was copper. The two towns were not at the same location; the scant remains of the earlier Silverbell are down the dirt road you'll be riding.

Follow the pavement around past the Silver Bell Mine to the dirt road that heads west. Leave your vehicle here and follow the road, which will go around behind the huge dumps of the modern mine. At 3.5 miles you'll cross a volcanic-looking slag dump from an old smelter. Then, at 5.7 miles, you'll see a small turnoff to your left. Take it to go to the old Silverbell Cemetery. At almost .6 miles beyond that fork, you'll come to another fork. Take a left down a sandy lane and within about .1 miles you'll come to the cemetery. Retrace your route back to the main road. When you reach the main road again, you can look across the draw to the workings of the first town named Silverbell (elev. 2450'). You can see adits (mine openings), waste dumps, and a few roads connecting the old mines.

If you went to the cemetery, your mileage back at the fork should be about 6.9. You have almost 13 miles to go to Sasco. Many of these miles will be on the roadbed of the Arizona and Southern Railroad, which carried ore from Silverbell to the smelter at Sasco and then on to the Southern Pacific's main line at Red Rock. The tracks were taken up in 1934, but I have seen railroad spikes just about every time I have been on the roadbed.

Exploring Sasco — The ghost town's name is an acronym for the Southern Arizona Smelting Company, which processed the ore for Silverbell and the nearby Picacho Mines beginning in 1907. The smelter closed for good just after the end of World War I. There's a lot to see in this desert site; part of the challenge is to look at the huge foundations and try to imagine what the place looked like when it was operating.

You'll know you're nearing Sasco (elev. 1820') when a large power line crosses the old roadbed you've been riding from Silverbell. To your left a branch of the old railroad leaves your main road. Just before it is a large concrete pit that I'm guessing was used to work on railroad cars and/or engines. Shortly after that, on your right, is a road that goes to several foundations and an old stone fountain.

The main road continues northeast and gets a bit rough as it cuts through a hill. Immediately afterwards, take the left into the main smelter site. You'll see huge foundations, the smelter stack foundation (with "Sasco, '07" in the concrete), a large slag pile, and other remnants of the operation. If you look around carefully enough, you'll find the railroad platform that still says "Sasco" in concrete.

East of the smelter are three items worth riding to: the "city hall," which looks more like a jail; the stone remains of the Rockland Hotel; and, farther northeast, the Sasco Cemetery, across the road from La Osa Ranch. Many of those buried there died in the influenza epidemic of 1919.

Version Two — One way from Silver Bell to Sasco or Red Rock

I'd like to try this, because when we rode from Silver Bell to Sasco, we knew we'd have a long return trip with more uphill than down, so we didn't ride the Sasco area the way we would have liked. But if someone had met us either in Sasco or in Red Rock (on I-10) we could have explored Sasco (and avoided an uphill return).

Version Three — Riding Sasco and Environs

I've done this perhaps ten times. We go to Red Rock (elev. 1860') and drive west 3 miles to the intersection beyond the cattle pens. We then ride the 3.3 miles to Sasco. We visit the cemetery, all the buildings and foundations of the site, and then we head out on the back roads and trails, of which there are miles. Here are a few favorites (the Samaniego Hills map gives a clearer picture):

1. From the cemetery, head west for about 2.5 miles (watch for dogs at the one residence). A road then circumnavigates the twin

The smelter stack base at Sasco

peaks to the north and returns to the intersection where the residence is. Or you can go right just past the water tank and cut over to the straight east-west road.

2. Take that same east-west road from the cemetery and turn left at the main gate where there is a road going south (be sure to shut the gate). Ride south to the power line trail and either take it back to Sasco or continue south; both routes will return to the Sasco Road.

3. Try some of the roads that go south from the Sasco Road. Two good ones leave near the power lines. One, west of the line, goes to a water catchment for wildlife. Another, east of the first road, passes under the power line and heads off towards the Samaniego Mountains. And a third road winds around through washes to some beautiful petroglyphs, but I'll be intentionally vague about that one.

Sasco's Rockland Hotel

Ride Eight — Kitt Peak via The Old Road

Level of Difficulty — *Tough and more tough*
Topographic Map — *1979 Kitt Peak 7.5'*

Kitt Peak from base to top by road bike is a challenging 9-mile climb that rises from 3229' to 6720'. The mountain bike version makes the same climb taking a terrible road for seven miles on a route recommended only for very experienced riders.

Where the paved road starts its western bend at the base of Kitt Peak (elev. 3620), the old road takes off in dirt. After about a mile, you'll have to lift your bike over a chain across the road (when I went, there was no sign prohibiting entry). The term "road" becomes relative from now on: it has been abandoned, so brush grows on the route and slides have eroded the trail. The climb also becomes extremely steep, with grades of up to 17%. We were able to stay on our bikes, although we did take frequent water breaks.

For the last mile of the route the road is maintained and faster going. I strongly suggest taking the 9-mile paved road down the mountain back to your car, as the downhill on the old road could be extremely hazardous because of its generally poor condition. Besides, the paved downhill is effortless, and you've earned a break.

Ride Nine — The Cochran Charcoal Kilns

Level of Difficulty — *not technical, uphill return*
Topographic Map — *1964 North Butte 7.5'; 1966 Ninety-*
Six Hills NW 7.5'; 1966 Ninety-Six Hills NE 7.5'

Here's a desert ride that has as its turnaround point the lovely Gila River and features one of Arizona's more startling sights — a view of the charcoal kilns at Cochran.

[Caution: This is not a hot weather ride. Be sure to have plenty of food and water, as no facilities exist along the route.]

Drive to Florence and head east on the road that forms the northern side of the state prison. After about 16.7 miles you'll see a large outcropping of rocks to the north and a dirt road heading past them. Park your car here (the road going south, incidentally, is Willow Springs Road, which comes out on state route 77 between Oracle and Oracle Junction and is a pleasant route to ride or drive).

Ride north on the dirt road (beginning elevation 2690') for 12.7 miles. You'll have a lot of rollercoaster hills, some agreeable downhills, and a bit of wash riding. Eventually you'll top a rise (about 11.5 miles from your car) where you can see the riparian habitation of the Gila River. Scan the western hills across the river (this would be a

The Cochran Charcoal Kilns

great ride to take binoculars along) for one of Arizona's most impressive back roads sights: five "beehive" charcoal kilns, used to convert wood to charcoal through controlled high-temperature heating.

Continue down to the water (your elevation at this point is 1643', or 1047 feet lower than your point of origin). The Gila River is a beautiful, cool change of pace from the desert, and we spent a lot of time at the water, probably because we knew when we left we'd have considerable climbing to do.

Cochran, a town of about a hundred people, stood near the spot where the road crosses the railroad tracks. It had a post office from 1905 to 1915 with John S. Cochran, who named the town after himself, as postmaster. The town was built for the railroad, although it also served the mines in the area.

Ride Ten — Copper Creek

Level of Difficulty — moderately difficult to very technical
Topographic Maps — 1948 (photorevised 1972) Mammoth 7.5'; 1948 (photorevised 1972) Clark Ranch 7.5'; 1949 (photo- inspected 1972) Holy Joe Peak 7.5'; 1972 Oak Grove Canyon 7.5'; 1972 Rhodes Peak 7.5'

The Galiuro Mountains are relatively close to Tucson and yet are much less frequented by our fellow humans than are the Rincons, Catalinas, or Santa Ritas. And in the Galiuros, up in a scenic canyon, stands an old abandoned ghost town with mining remnants, a running stream, and even a roofless stone mansion. Tempted?

For this route I'd recommend a sturdy truck or, even better, a four-wheel drive vehicle. Take it to Mammoth, 39 miles northeast of the intersection of Ina and Oracle roads on the northwest side of Tucson. In downtown Mammoth, find the intersection of Main and Bluebird. Go east on Bluebird, which becomes a dirt road, to cross the San Pedro River wash. Usually it's dry and quite passable, but if it isn't, you can use a detour: if the San Pedro is running, go north on state route 77 out of town and cross the river by bridge. Then turn right .5 miles past the bridge and head south for 2.3 miles. At that point, the extension of Bluebird that crosses the San Pedro and the paved bypass meet. At that intersection, just a few feet north of where the paved roads meet at a "T", a dirt road heads east. That is Copper Creek Road (elev. 2384' at this point).

Copper Creek Road will follow a wash for a short distance and then climb up onto a plateau. For about 6 miles the road will be wide and easy to traverse. Then it will take a sharp drop into a ravine where you can see some ranch buildings below. For standard trucks, the top of this ravine (elev. 3967') should be the end of the road and the mountain bikes should come out. Four-wheel drive vehicles, of course, can continue, but I think that if it's great mountain biking that brought you here, it's time to go two-wheeling anyway. It's about 2.7 miles of rough roads and creek crossings to the main townsite. [*Warning: If Copper Creek is running swiftly, do not attempt to cross it.]* Along the way, in the spectacular narrow canyon cut by Copper Creek, you'll see ample evidence of the mining efforts: tailings, foundations, a bridge, and the bed of a narrow gauge railroad.

When you leave the stream and make one short, steep climb, you'll come to the site of the old post office and general store (elev. 4010'). There, set into the rocks, is a concrete sign proclaiming the town's name. Copper Creek was founded in the 1860s but didn't get a post office until 1907. One source says that the site had over 50

Store and office building across Copper Creek from the mansion

buildings and that two hundred miners and their families lived here. The mines were dormant from 1917 until 1933; the post office closed in 1942.

Now the Rhodes Peak and Oak Grove Canyon topographic maps can really help you. Continue east past the foundations, dropping down to the creek. Cross the water and pass the old dam on the right. Keep going. When the road crosses Copper Creek again, you have two choices. What you want to see are the "ruins" marked on the Oak Grove topo map near benchmark ("BM ") 4245. A trail leads up the creek from this point that I have walked but not ridden. But I have ridden the jeep road that leads up the canyon wall. You will take a left after a very steep hill and follow that rough road back down to Copper Creek. With either route, in just about 1.5 miles, you'll come to the stunning "Mansion at Copper Creek."

Built between 1908 and 1910 by Indian labor, the twenty-room mansion, which is about 100 feet square, once featured a second story balcony, a huge picture window, hand polished wood floors, and a patio with a fruit orchard. The estate was built by Roy Sibley, manager of the Minnesota-Arizona Mining Company, which owned the claims on Copper Creek. His wife, Belle, was supposed to have been rather culture conscious, and this showplace residence was her attempt to civilize the mining camp. Roy Sibley owned a Stutz Bearcat, and he had a road crew whose sole job it was to keep the road open from Copper Creek to the outside world. That road, incidentally, is not the one you came in on: The orginal access was from Willcox to Aravaipa Valley to the head of Copper Creek — a distance of some 75 miles. Across the creek from the mansion stands a long stone building that housed two offices with a store between them. Nearby are scant remains of an adobe building.

The Sibley Mansion on Copper Creek

notes